MW00364366

SAY IT IN
SPANISH
NEW EDITION

JOYCE PUEBLA

DOVER PUBLICATIONS, INC.
Mineola, New York

Bibliographical Note

This Dover edition, first published in 2011, is a completely
revised and updated work, which supersedes the book of
the same title originally published in 1960.

Library of Congress Cataloging-in-Publication Data

Puebla, Joyce.
   Say it in Spanish / Joyce Puebla. — New ed.
      p. cm.
   "Completely revised and updated work, which super-
sedes the book of the same title originally published in
1960."
   Includes index.
   ISBN-13: 978-0-486-47634-6
   ISBN-10: 0-486-47634-0
   1. Spanish language—Conversation and phrase books.
I. Title.
PC4121.P83 2011
468.3'421—dc22

                                          2011015700

Manufactured in the United States by Courier Corporation
47634001
www.doverpublications.com

Contents

CONTENTS

CONTENTS

Quick & to the Point/Sidebars

Throughout the book, you will notice two types of shaded boxes. The "Quick & to the Point" sections summarize the most important words and phrases contained in the chapter. These essential and handy phrases provide the easiest and simplest communication that a traveler may need on any given topic. The sidebars, also appearing in tinted boxes, contain an interesting fact for the traveler. Pertinent to the theme of each chapter, the sidebars may inform readers about a unique aspect of the culture, feature special details about the language, or offer a bit of entertaining trivia.

Scheme of Pronunciation

The difficulty of pronunciation of Spanish for an American arises mainly from the difference in the pronunciation of the vowels. English vowels can be pronounced several different ways. In Spanish vowels have only one sound. Vowel sounds are shorter than in English and are never drawn out.

The pronunciation in this book should be read simply as in English with the stress placed upon the syllables in capital letters. In this book we are using the following letters to represent the Spanish pronunciation.

a	*ah* as in *drama*
e	*eh* as in *set*
i	*ee* as in *bee*
o	*oh* as in *no*
u	*oo* as in *moon*
ai, ay	*i* as in *pie*
au	*ow* as in *cow*
oi, oy	*oy* as in *toy*
ue	*weh* as in *went*
ui	*wee* as in *we*

SCHEME OF PRONUNCIATION

Spanish consonants are mostly similar to English with the following exceptions.

b and **v** sound alike in Spanish—like a soft *b*.

c followed by i or e sounds like the *th* in *thin* in Spain and like the *s* in *say* elsewhere. Followed by *aou* it has a hard *k* sound.

d is much softer than the English *d*. It is close to the *th* sound in English.

h is always silent; it is never pronounced.

j and **g** (when followed by i or e) is like a spitty, guttural *h*.

ll is pronounced like the *y* in yellow. (This varies in some Spanish-speaking countries.)

ñ is pronounced like the *ny* in *canyon*.

qu is always a hard *k* sound as in *key*.

rr and r at the beginning of a word is trilled or rolled. It isn't a sound we have in English, so it requires some practice.

x is pronounced like *x* in *taxi* when it appears between two vowels and like the *s* in *say* when it is followed by a consonant.

z sounds like the *th* in *thin* in Spain and like the *s* in *say* in many other Spanish-speaking countries.

SAY IT IN
SPANISH
NEW EDITION

Quick & to the Point

Yes. No. Perhaps. Sí. No. Puede ser. *see. noh.*
PWEH-deh sehr.

Please. Por favor. *pohr fah-BOHR.*

Excuse me. (To get someone's attention if I have a question)
Disculpe. *dehs-KOOL-peh.*

Excuse me. (If someone is in my way or I need to squeeze through)
Con permiso. *kohn pehr-MEE-soh.*

Excuse me. (If I bump into someone) Perdón. *pehr-DOHN.*

Thanks (very much). (Muchas) gracias.
(MOO-chahs) GRAH-see-ahs.

You're welcome. No hay de que *or* De nada.
noh I deh keh or deh NAH-dah.

Don't mention it! ¡No faltaba más! *noh fahl-TAH-bah mahs.*

Welcome! ¡Bienvenidos! *bee-ehn-beh-NEE-dohs!*

Restrooms. Los servicios *or* los aseos.
lohs sehr-BEE-see-ohs or lohs ah-SEH-ohs.

Ladies' room. Damas *or* Señoras *or* Mujeres.
DAH-mahss or seh- NYO-rahss or moo-HEH-rehs.

Men's room. Caballeros *or* Señores *or* Hombres.
kah-bah-YEH-rohss or seh-NYOH-rehs or OHM-brehs.

Useful Expressions/*Expresiones Útiles*

1. **Do you speak (a little) English?**
   ¿Habla usted (un poco de) inglés?
   AH-blah oos-TEHD (oon POH-koh deh) een-GLEHS?

2. **I speak only English (French).**
   Sólo hablo inglés (francés).
   SOH-loh AH-bloh een-GLEHS (frahn-SEHS).

3. **German, Italian.** Alemán, italiano.
   ah-leh-MAHN, ee-tah-lee-AH-noh.

4. **I am from the United States.**
   Soy de los Estados Unidos.
   soy deh lohs eys-TAH-dohs oo-NEE-dohs.

5. **My mailing address is_____.**
   Mi dirección (postal) es _____.
   mee dee-rehk-see-OHN (pohs-TAHL) ehs _____.

6. **My email address is Mary@(at)abc. (dot) com**
   Mi dirección de correo electrónico es Mary @
   (arroba) abc. (punto) com.
   *mee dee-rehk-see-OHN deh koh-REH-oh eh-lehk-
   TROH-nee-koh ehs Mary ah-RROH-bah ah beh seh
   POON-toh kohm.*

7. **He (she) is from_____.** Él (ella) es de _____.
   ehl (EH-yah) ehs deh _____.

8. **Could you please speak a little slower?**
   ¿Puede hablar un poco más despacio, por favor?
   *PWEH-deh ah-BLAHR oon POH-koh mahs dehs-PAH-
   see-oh, pohr fah-BOHR?*

1

9. **I (don't) understand.** (No) comprendo.
   (noh) kohm-PREHN-doh.

10. **Could you repeat it, please?**
    ¿Puede repetirlo, por favor?
    PWEH-deh rreh-peh-TEER-loh, pohr fah-BOHR.

11. **Again.** Otra vez. *OH-trah behs.*

12. **Write it down, please.** Escríbalo, por favor.
    ehs-KREE-bah-loh, pohr fah-BOHR.

13. **What do you wish?** ¿Qué desea usted?
    keh de-SEH-ah oos-TED?

14. **How much is it?** ¿Cuánto es? *KWAHN-toh ehs?*

15. **Come here. Come in.** Venga acá. Pase usted.
    BEHN-gah ah-KAH. PAH-seh oos-TEHD.

16. **Wait a moment.** Espere un momento.
    ehs-PEH-reh oon moh-MEHN-toh.

17. **Why? When?** ¿Por qué? ¿Cuándo?
    por KEH, KWAHN-doh?

18. **How? How long?** ¿Cómo? ¿Cuánto tiempo?
    KOH-moh? KWAHN-toh tee-EHM-poh?

19. **Who? What?** ¿Quién? ¿Qué? *kee-EHN? keh?*

20. **Where is _____?** ¿Dónde está?
    DOHN-deh ehs-TAH?

21. **Here, there.** Aquí, allí. *ah-KEE, ah-YEE.*

22. **It is (not) all right.** (No) está bien.
    (noh) ehss-TA bee-EHN.

23. It is old (new). Es viejo (nuevo).
ehs bee-EH-hoh (NWEH-boh).

24. Empty, full. Vacío, lleno. *bah-SEE-oh, YEH-noh.*

25. That is (not) all. Eso (no) es todo.
EH-so (noh) ehs TOH-doh.

26. To, from, with. A, de, con. *ah, deh, kohn.*

27. In, on, near, far. En, sobre, cerca de, lejos de.
ehn, SOH-breh, SEHR-kah deh, LEH-hohs deh.

28. In front of, behind. Enfrente de, detrás de.
en-FREHN-teh deh, DEH-trahs deh.

29. Beside, inside, outside.
Al lado de, dentro de, fuera de.
ahl LAH-doh deh, DEHN-troh deh, FWEH-rah deh.

30. Something, nothing. Algo, nada. *AHL-goh, NAH-dah.*

31. Several, few. Algunos, pocos.
ahl-GOO-nohs, POH-kohs.

32. More or less. Más o menos. *mahs oh MEH-nohs.*

33. A little. Un poquito. *oon poh-KEE-toh.*

34. Enough, too much. Suficiente, demasiado.
soo-fee-see-EHN-teh, deh-mah-see-AH-doh.

35. Much, many. Mucho, muchos.
MOO-choh, MOO-chohs.

36. Good, better (than). Bueno, mejor (que).
BWEH-noh, meh-HOHR (keh).

37. Bad, worse (than). Malo, peor (que).
MAH-lo, peh-OHR (keh).

38. Now, immediately.   Ahora, en seguida.
ah-OH-rah, ehn seh-GHEE-dah.

39. Soon, later.   Pronto, más tarde.
PROHN-toh, mahs TAHR-deh.

40. As soon as possible.   Lo más pronto posible.
loh mahs PROHN-toh poh-SEE-bleh.

41. At the latest.   A más tardar.   *ah mahss tahr-DAHR.*

42. At least.   Por los menos.   *pohr loh MEH-nohs.*

43. It is (very) late.   Es (muy) tarde.
ehs (mwee) TAHR-deh.

44. It is early.   Es temprano.   *ehss tehm-PRAH-noh*

45. Slowly, slower.   Despacio, más despacio.
dehs-PAH-see-oh, mahs dehss-PAH-see-oh.

46. Quickly, faster.   Aprisa, más aprisa.
ah-PREE-sah, mahs ah PREE-sah.

47. I am (not) in a hurry.   (No) tengo prisa.
(noh) TEN-goh PREE-sah.

48. I am warm (cold).   Tengo calor (frío).
TEHN-goh kah-LOHR (FREE-oh).

49. Hungry, thirsty, sleepy.   Hambre, sed, sueño.
AHM-breh, sehd, SWEH-nyoh.

50. I am busy (tired, ill).
Estoy ocupado (cansado, enfermo).   *ehs-TOY oh-
koo-PAH-doh (kahn-SAH-doh, ehn-FEHR-moh).*

51. What is the matter here?   ¿Qué pasa aquí?
keh PAH-sah ah-KEE?

52. Help! Fire! Thief! ¡Socorro! ¡Fuego! ¡Ladrón!
soh-KOH-rroh! FWEH-goh! lah-DROHN!

53. Look out! ¡Cuidado! *kwee-DAH-doh!*

54. Listen. Look here. Oiga. Mire. *OY-gah. MEE-reh.*

55. Can you help (tell) me?
¿Puede usted ayudarme (decirme) _____?
PWEH-deh oos-TEHD ah-yoo-DAHR-meh (deh-SEER-meh) _____?

56. I'm looking for _____. Busco _____. *BOOS-koh.*

57. I would like _____. Quisiera _____.
kee-see-EHR-ah _____.

58. Can you recommend a _____?
¿Puede usted recomendar un _____? *PWEH-deh
oos-TEHD rreh-koh-mehn-DAHR oon _____.*

59. Do you want _____? ¿Desea usted _____?
deh-SEH-ah oos-TEHD _____?

60. I am (very) glad. Me alegro (mucho).
meh ah-LEH-groh (MOO-choh)

61. I am sorry. Lo siento. *loh see-EHN-toh.*

62. It is (not) my fault. (No) es mi culpa.
(noh) ehs mee KOOL-pah.

63. Whose fault is it? ¿Quién tiene la culpa?
kee-EHN tee-EH-neh lah KOOL-pah?

64. I (don't) know. (No) sé. *(no) seh.*

65. I (don't) think so. Creo que sí. (no).
KREH-oh keh see (noh).

Exclamations/Exclamaciones

Good luck! ¡Buena suerte! *BWEH-nah SWEHR-teh!*

Great! ¡Chévere! *CHE-beh-reh!*

Oh, dear me! ¡Ay! *i!*

Look. Mira. *MEE-rah.*

Really? ¿De veras? *deh BEH-rahs?*

Cheers! God bless you! (after a sneeze). ¡Salud! *sah-LOOD!*

Okay. De acuerdo, bien. *deh ah-KWEHR-doh, bee-EHN.*

Okay. Vale. *BAH-leh.*

What a pity! ¡Qué lástima¡ *keh LAHS-tee-mah!*

Let's go! ¡Vamos! *BAH-mohs!*

Bye! ¡Hasta luego! *AHS-tah loo-eh-goh!*

Of course, for sure! ¡Claro! *klah-roh!*

No way! ¡Ni pensarlo!, ¡Qué va! *nee pehn-SAHR-loh!, keh vah!*

Do what you like! ¡Haz lo que quieras! *ahs loh keh kee-EH-rahs!*

My gosh! ¡Dios mío! *dee-OHS MEE-oh!*

Listen! ¡Oye! *OH-yeh!*

How odd! ¡Qué raro! *keh RAH-roh!*

66. What is that for? ¿Para qué es eso?
PAH-rah keh ehs EH-so?

67. How do you say this in Spanish?
¿Cómo se dice esto en español? *KOH-moh seh
DEE-seh EHS-toh ehn eh- pah-NYOHL?*

68. How do you say _____? ¿Cómo se dice _____?
KOH-moh seh DEE-seh _____?

69. How do you spell "antiguo"?
¿Cómo se deletrea "antiguo"?
KOH-moh seh deh-leh-TREH-ah ahn-TEE-gwoh?

Difficulties/Las Dificultades

70. I cannot find my hotel address.
No puedo hallar la dirección de mi hotel.
*noh PWEH-doh ah-YAHR lah dee-rehk-see-OHN deh
mee oh-TEHL.*

Quick & to the Point

Stop, thief! ¡Detengan al ladrón! *deh-TEHN-gahn ahl
lah-DROHN!*

Emergency. Emergencia. *eh-mehr-HEHN-see-ah.*

Police. Policía. *poh-lee-SEE-ah.*

Help. Ayuda. *ah-YOO-dah.*

Call a doctor. Llamen a un médico. *YAH-mehn ah oon
MEH-dee-koh.*

Fire! ¡Fuego! *fweh-goh!*

7

71. I don't remember the name of the street.
No recuerdo cómo se llama la calle.   *noh rreh-KWEHR-doh KOH-moh seh YAH-mah lah KAH-yeh.*

72. I can't find my friends.   No encuentro a mis amigos.
noh ehn-KWEHN-troh ah mees ah-MEE-gohs.

73. I left my purse (wallet) in _____.
Dejé mi bolsa (mi cartera) en _____.   *de-HEH mee BOHL-sah (mee kahr-TEH-rah) ehn _____.*

74. I forgot my money (key).   Olvidé mi dinero (llave).
ohl-bee-DEH mee dee-NEH roh (YAH-beh).

75. I have missed my train (plane).
He perdido mi tren (avión).
eh-pehr-DEE-doh mee trehn. (ah-bee-OHN).

76. What am I to do?   ¿Qué debo hacer?
keh DEH-bo ah-SEHR.

77. You said it would cost _____.
Usted dijo que costaría _____.   *oos-TED DEE-ho keh kohs-tah-REE-ah _____.*

78. They are bothering me (us).
Ellos me (nos) molestan.
EH-yohs meh (nohs) moh-LES-tahn.

79. Go away.   Váyase.   *BAH-yah-seh.*

80. I will call a policeman.   Llamaré a un policía.
yah-mah-REH ah oon poh-lee-SEE-ah.

81. I have been robbed of _____.
Me han robado _____.
meh ahn rro-BAH-doh _____.

Common Sayings

Folk wisdom in Spanish   Refranes

That's life!   ¡Así es la vida!

What will be, will be!   ¡Que será, será!

Better late than never.   Más vale tarde que nunca.

My house is your house.   Mi casa es su casa.

Beggars can't be choosers.   Hay buen hambre, no hay pan duro. (There's no hard bread to someone who is hungry.

Time cures all.   El tiempo lo cura todo.

You can judge a man by the company he keeps.   Dime con quién andas, y te dire quién eres. (Tell me with whom you walk, and I will tell you who you are.)

A friend in need is a friend indeed.   En las malas se conocen a los amigos. (In bad times, you know your friends.

Bad things happen in threes.   No hay dos sin tres. (There are no twos without threes.)

Try your tricks somewhere else.   A otro perro con ese hueso. (To another dog with that bone.)

82. Where is the police station?

¿Dónde está la estación de policía? *DOHN-deh es-TAH la es-tah-see-OHN-deh poh-lee-SEE-ah?*

83. The Lost and Found Desk.

La sección de objetos perdidos. *la sehk-see-OHN deh ohb-HEH-tohs pehr-DEE-dohs.*

Greetings, Introductions, etc./Saludos, Presentaciones, etc.

84. What is your name _____?

¿Cómo se llama usted? *KOH-moh seh YAH-mah oos TEHD?*

Quick & to the Point

Good morning, good day. Buenos días, buen día. *BWEH-nohs DEE-ahs, BWEN DEE-ah.*

Good afternoon. Buenas tardes. *BWEH-nahs TAHR-dehs.*

Good evening, Good night. Buenas noches. *BWEH-nahs NOH-chehs.*

Goodbye. Until next time. Adiós. Hasta la próxima vez. *ah-dee-OHS. AHS-tah lah PROHK-see-mah behs.*

Bye! ¡Chau! *Chahw!*

Hello. Hola. *OH-lah.*

Hi, how's it going? How are you? (informal) ¿Qué tal? *kee-tahl?*

My name is _____. Me llamo _____. *meh YAH-moh _____.*

---

85. **May I introduce Mr. _____, Mrs. _____, Miss _____.**
Permítame presentar al señor _____, a la señora
_____, a la señorita _____. *pehr-MEE-tah-meh
preh-sehn-TAHR ahl seh-NYOHR _____, ah lah seh-
NYOH-rah _____, ah lah seh-NYOH-ree-tah _____.*

86. **My wife, my husband.** Mi esposa, mi esposo.
mee ehs-POH-sah, mee ehs-POH-soh.

87. **My daughter, my son.** Mi hija, mi hijo.
mee EE-hah, mee EE-hoh.

88. **My friend.** Mi amigo, mi amiga.
mee ah-MEE-goh, mee ah-MEE-gah.

89. **My sister, my brothers.** Mi hermana, mis hermanos.
mee ehr-MAH-nah, mees ehr-MAH-nohs.

90. **Charmed (to meet you).** Encantado/a.
ehn kahn-TAH-doh/dah.

91. **I am very glad to meet you.** Mucho gusto.
MOO-choh GOOS-toh.

92. **The pleasure is mine.** Igualmente.
ee-gwahl-MEHN-teh.

93. **How are you?** ¿Cómo está usted?
KOH-moh ehs-TAH oos-TEHD?

94. **Fine, thanks. And you?** Muy bien, gracias.
¿Y usted? *mwee bee-EHN, GRAH-see-ahs. ee oos-TEHD?*

95. **How is your family?** ¿Cómo está su familia?
KOH-moh ehs-TAH soo fah-MEE-lee-ah?

96. (Not) very well, thanks. (No) muy bien, gracias.
(noh) mwee bee-EHN, GRAH-see-ahs.

97. Please sit down. Por favor siéntese.
pohr fah-BOHR see-EHN-teh-seh.

98. I had a wonderful time. Me he divertido mucho.
meh eh dee-behr-TEE-doh MOO-cho.

99. I hope to see you again (soon).
Espero verle otra vez (pronto).
ehs-PEH-roh BEHR-leh OH-trah behs (PROHN-toh).

100. Come to see me (to see us).
Venga a verme (vernos).
BEHN-gah ah BEHR-meh (BEHR-nohs).

101. Are you free this afternoon (this evening)?
¿Está usted libre esta tarde (noche)?
ehs-TAH oos-TEHD LEE-breh EHS-tah TAHR-deh (EHS-tah NOH-cheh)?

102. Please give me your address.
Por favor deme su dirección.
pohr fah-BOHR DEH-meh soo dee-rehk-see-OHN.

103. Give my (our) regards to _____.
Por favor dé mis (nuestros) recuerdos a _____.
pohr fah-BOHR deh mees (noo-EHS-trohs) rreh-KWEHR-dohs ah _____.

104. I am (We are) going to _____.
Voy (Vamos) a _____. *boy (BAH-mohs) ah _____.*

Kisses and Hugs/*Besos y Abrazos*

Learning to speak Spanish involves more than just words. Gestures and customs vary in different countries, so learning this part of communication is important, too. Spanish-speaking people commonly greet each other with a quick, relaxed handshake that may be followed with a hug as they pat each other on the back. Women and young girls often greet each other with a quick kiss on the cheek, or both cheeks, depending on the local custom. This may also be followed between men and women who are friends. These gestures are often repeated when saying goodbye. Watch the people around you as you travel to observe how they greet each other.

Travel. General Expressions/*El Viaje. Expresiones Generales*

105. Is this the (direct) way to _____?
¿Es éste el camino (directo) a _____? *ehs EHS-teh ehl kah-MEE-noh (dee-REHK-toh) ah _____?*

106. How long will it take to go?
¿En cuánto tiempo se llega? *ehn KWAH-toh tee-EHM-poh seh YEH-gah?*

107. Where do I turn? ¿Dónde doy vuelta? *DOHN-deh doy BWEHL-tah?*

13

Quick & to the Point

Where is _____? ¿Dónde está _____?
DOHN-deh ehs-TAH _____?

I'm going to _____. Voy a _____. *boy ah _____.*

To the left, to the right. A la izquierda, a la derecha.
ah lah ees-kee EHR-dah, ah lah deh-REH-chah.

street.	la calle.	*lah KAH-yeh.*
avenue.	la avenida.	*lah ah-beh-NEE-dah.*
blocks.	las cuadras.	*lahs KWAH-drahs.*
corner.	la esquina.	*lah ehs-KEE-nah.*

108. To the north, south. Al norte, al sur.
Ahl NOHR-teh, ahl soor.

109. From the east, west. Del este, del oeste.
dehl EHS-teh, dehl oh-EHS-teh.

110. Straight ahead. Adelante or todo derecho.
Ah-dehl-AHN-teh, or TOH-doh deh-REH-choh.

111. Forward, backward. Adelante, atrás.
ah- deh-LAHN-teh, ah-TRAHS.

112. Turn left (right).
Doble a la izquierda (a la derecha). *DOH-bleh ah lah ees-kee-EHR-dah, ah lah deh-REH-chah.*

113. Cross the street. Cruce la calle.
KROO-seh lah KAH-yeh.

114. What street is this? ¿Qué calle es esta?
keh KAH-yeh ehs EHS-tah?

115. Circle, avenue, square.
El círculo, la avenida, la plaza.
ehl SEER-koo-loh, lah ah-beh-NEE-dah, lah PLAH-sah.

116. Two blocks ahead. Dos cuadras de frente.
dohs KWAH-drahs deh FREH-teh.

117. Is it far from/near here? ¿Está lejos/cerca de aquí?
eh-STAH LEH-hohs/SEHR-kah deh ah-KEE?

118. Can you show me on a map?
¿Lo puede mostrar en el mapa?
loh PWEH-deh mohs-TRAHR ehn ehl MAH-pah?

119. Can I walk there? ¿Se puede ir andando?
seh PWEH-deh eer ahn-DAHN-doh?

Things you may hear./*Cosas que puede escuchar.*

Okay! ¡De acuerdo! *deh ah-KWEHR-doh!*
Sure! ¡Claro! *CLAH-roh!*
Let's go. Vámonos. *BAH-mah-nohs.*
Wait. Espera. *eh-SPEHR-ah.*
Wait a second. Espera un segundo.
eh-SPEHR-ah oon seh-GOON-doh.
Are you ready? ¿Estás listo/a? *ehs-TAHS LEES-toh/tah?*
I'm ready. Estoy listo/a. *ehs-TOY LEE-stoh/stah.*
Careful! ¡Ojo! *OH-hoh!*
Follow me. Sígueme. *SEE-geh-meh.*

15

120. Please point. Por favor indicar.
pohr fah-BOHR een-dee-KAHR.

121. The airport. El aeropuerto.
ehl ah-eh-roh PWEHR-toh.

122. The bus station (stop).
La estación de autobuses (la parada de auto-
búses). *lah ehs-tah-see-OHN deh ahw-toh BOO-
sehs (lah pah-RAH-dah deh ahw-toh-BOO-sehs).*

123. The dock. El muelle. *Ehl MWEH-yeh.*

124. The railway station. La estación de trenes.
lah ehs-tah-cee-OHN deh TREH-nehs.

125. The taxi stand. La parada de taxis.
lah pah-RAH-dah deh TAHK-sees.

126. The metro station. La estación de metros.
lah ehs-tah-see-OHN deh MEH-trohs.

127. The platform. El andén. *ehl ahn-DEHN.*

128. Cross the road at the next corner, at the traffic light.
Cruce la calle en la próxima esquina, en el semáforo. *KROO-seh lah-KAH-yeh ehn lah PROHK-see-
moh ehs-KEE-nah, ehn ehl seh-MAH-foh-roh.*

Airplane/El Avión

129. Is there motor service to the airport?
¿Hay servicio de transporte al aeropuerto? *i sehr-
vee-SEE-oh deh trahns-POHR-teh ahl ah-eh-roh-
PWEHR-toh?*

130. At what time will they come for me?

¿A qué hora vienen por mí?

ah keh OH-rah bee-EH-nehn pohr mee?

131. When is there a plane to _____?

¿A qué hora sale el avión para _____? *ah keh OH-rah SAH-leh ehl ah-bee-OHN PAH-rah _____?*

132. Is food served on the plane?

¿Se sirve comida en el avión? *seh SEER-veh koh-MEE-dah ehn ehl ah-bee-OHN?*

133. I require a kosher (vegetarian) meal.

Deseo una comida kosher (vegetariana). *deh-SEH-oh OO-nah koh-MEE-dah KOH-shehr (beh-heh-tah-ree-AH-nah).*

Quick & to the Point

Baggage. El equipaje. *ehl eh-kee-PAH-heh.*

Boarding pass. El pase de abordar.
ehl PAH-seh deh ah-bohr-DAHR.

Ticket. El pasaje, el billete. *ehl pah-SAH-heh, ehl bee-YEH-teh.*

Departure gate. La puerta de embarque.
lah PWEHR-tah deh ehm-BAHR-keh.

Departures. Salidas. *sah-LEE-dahs.*

Baggage claim ticket. El talón de equipaje.
ehl tah-LOHN deh eh-kee-PAH-heh.

Arrivals. Llegadas. *yeh-GAH-dahs.*

134. How much baggage may I take?

¿Cuántos kilos de equipaje puedo llevar?
KWAHN-tohs KEE-lohs deh eh-kee-PAH-heh PWEH-doh yeh-BAHR?

135. I want to go to the airline office.

Quiero ir a la oficina de la línea aérea. *KEE—ehr oh eer ah lah oh-fee-SEE-nah deh lah LEE-neh-ah ah-EH-reh-ah.*

136. The ticket office. La taquilla. *lah tah-KEE-yah.*

137. A ticket, a timetable. Un billete, un horario.
oon bee-YEH-teh, oon oh RAH-ree-oh.

138. A porter. Un portero. *oon pohr-TEH-roh.*

139. The baggage room. La sala de equipajes.
lah SAH-lah deh eh-kee-PAH-hehs.

140. How does one go? ¿Por dónde se va?
pohr DOHN-deh seh vah?

141. When will we arrive at _____?

¿Cuándo llegaremos a _____?
KWAN-doh yeh-gah-REH-mohs ah _____?

Timetables in Spanish-speaking countries use the 24-hour clock to announce departure and arrival times. To read the schedule, just subtract 12 from the hour. For example, 18:30 would be 6:30 p.m. $(18 - 12 = 6)$.

142. Please call a taxi for me.

Por favor, llámeme un taxi.   *pohr fah-BOHR YAH-me-meh oon TAHK-see.*

143. Is this seat taken?   ¿Está reservado este asiento?
ehs-TAH reh-sehr-VAH-doh ES-teh ah-see-EHN-toh?

144. Can I reserve a (front) seat?

¿Puedo reservar un asiento (delantero)?
PWEH-doh reh-sehr-BAHR oon ah-see-EHN toh (deh-lahn-TEH-roh)?

145. A seat by the window.

Un asiento junto a la ventanilla.
oon ah-see-EHN-toh HOON-toh ah lah behn-tah-NEE-yah.

At Customs/En la Aduana

146. Where is customs?   ¿Dónde está la aduana?
DOHN-deh eh-STAH lah ah-DWAH-nah?

147. This is my baggage. _____pieces.
Este es mi equipaje. _____ piezas.
EHS-teh ehs mee eh-kee-PAH-heh. _____pee-EH-sahs.

148. Here is my passport.   Aquí tiene mi pasaporte.
ah-KEE tee-EH-neh mee pah-sah-POHR-teh.

149. Should I open everything?   ¿Debo abrir todo?
DEH-boh ah-BREER TOH-doh?

150. I cannot open that.   No puedo abrir ese.
noh PWEH-doh ah-BREER EH-seh.

Quick & to the Point

Passport.   Pasaporte.   *pah-sah-POHR-teh.*

What is the purpose of your visit?   ¿Cuál es el motivo de su viaje?
kwahl ehs ehl moh-TEE-boh deh soo bee-AH-heh?

How long do you plan to be in _____?
Por cuánto tiempo piensa estar en _____?
pohr KWAHN-toh tee-EHM-poh pee-EHN-sah ehs-TAHR en _____?

Do you have anything to declare?   ¿Tiene algo que declarar?
tee-EH-neh AHL-goh keh deh-klah-RAHR?

Customs.   Aduanas.   *ah-DWAH-nahs.*

151. I have lost the key.   Perdí la llave.
pehr-DEE lah YAH-beh.

152. I have nothing to declare.
No tengo nada que declarar.
noh TEHN-goh NAH-dah keh deh-clah-RAHR.

153. All of this is for my personal use.
Todo esto es para mi uso personal.   *TOH-doh EHS-toh ehs PAH-rah mee OO-soh pehr-soh-NAHL.*

154. There is nothing here but _____.
No hay más que _____.   *noh i mahs keh _____.*

155. These are gifts.   Estos son regalos.   *EHS-tohs sohn reh-GAH-lohs.*

156. Is there a duty to pay on these articles?
¿Hay que pagar impuestos sobre estos artículos?
i keh pah-GAHR eem-PWEHS-tohs SOH-breh EHS-tohs ahr-TEE-koo-lohs?

157. How much must I pay? ¿Cuánto tengo que pagar?
KWAHN-toh TEHN-goh keh pah-GAHR?

158. That is all I have. Eso es todo lo que tengo.
EH-soh ehs TOH-doh loh keh TEHN-goh.

159. Please be careful. Por favor, tenga cuidado.
pohr fah-BOHR, TEHN-gah kwee-DAH-doh.

160. Have you finished? ¿Ha terminado usted?
ah tehr-mee-NAH-doh oos-TEHD?

161. I cannot find my baggage.
Se me perdió el equipaje.
seh meh pehr-dee-OH ehl eh-kee-PAH-heh.

162. My train leaves in _____ minutes.
Mi tren sale en _____ minutos.
mee trehn SAH-leh ehn_____ mee-NOO-tohs.

Signs/Signos

Customs. Aduana. *ah-DWAHN-ah.*
Immigration. Inmigración.
een-mee grah-see-OHN.
Passport Control. Control de pasaporte.
cohn-TRHOL deh pas-ah-POHR-teh.
Duty Free Goods. Artículos Libres de Impuestos.
ahr-TEE-coo-lohs LEE-brehs deh eem-PUES-tohs.

21

Tickets/ Los Billetes

163. I would like to buy a ticket to _____.
Me gustaría comprar un billete a _____.
meh goos-tah-REE-ah kohm-PRAHR oon bee-YEH-teh ah _____.

164. How much does a ticket to Madrid cost?
¿Cuánto cuesta un billete a Madrid? *KWAHN-toh KWEHS-tah oon bee-YEH-teh ah mah-DREED?*

165. What time does the plane leave?
¿A qué hora sale el avión?
ah keh OHR-ah SAH-leh ehl ah-bee-OHN?

166. How much is a ticket to _____.
¿Cuánto cuesta un billete a _____?
KWAN-toh KWEHS-tah oon bee-YEH-teh ah _____?

167. One-way ticket. Un billete sencillo.
oon bee-YEH-teh sehn-SEE-yoh.

168. A round trip ticket. Un billete de ida y vuelta.
oon bee-YEH-teh deh EE-dah ee BWEHL-tah.

169. First-class, second-class, third-class.
Primera clase, segunda clase, tercera clase. *pree-MEH-rah KLAH-seh, seh-GOON-dah KLAH-seh, tehr-SEH-rah KLAH-seh.*

170. An adult/child/student/senior citizen fare.
Una tarifa de adulto/niño/ estudiante/jubilado.
OON-ah tah-REE-fah deh ah-DOOL-toh/NEE-nyo/ eh-stoo-dee-AHN-teh/hoo-bee-LAH-doh.

171. Can I go by way of _____?   ¿Puedo ir via _____?
   PWEH-doh eer BEE-ah?

172. How long is it good for?
   ¿Por cuántos días es bueno?
   pohr KWAHN-tohs DEE-ahs ehs BWEH-noh?

173. Can I get something to eat on the way?
   ¿Se puede comer en el camino?
   seh PWEH-deh KOH-mehr ehn ehl kah-MEE-noh?

174. How much baggage may I take?
   ¿Cuántos kilos de equipaje se permiten llevar?
   KWAN-tohs KEE-lohs deh eh-kee-PAH-heh seh pehr-MEE-tehn yeh-BAHR?

175. How much per kilogram for excess?
   ¿Cuánto por kilogramo por exceso?
   KWAN-toh pohr kee-loh-GRAH-moh pohr ehk-SEH-soh?

176. Is there travel insurance?
   ¿Hay seguro para viajeros?
   i seh-GOO-roh PAH-rah bee-ah-HEH-rohs?

177. I'd like to confirm (cancel, change) my reservation.
   Quisiera confirmar (cancelar, cambiar) mi reservación.
   kee-see-EH-rah kohn-feer-MAHR (kahn-seh-LAHR, kahm-bee-AHR) mee reh-sehr-bah-see-OHN.

178. It's full. Está lleno.   *eh-STAH YEH-noh.*

179. Is it completely full?   ¿Está completamente lleno?
   eh-STAH kohm-pleh-tah-MEHN-teh YEH-noh?

23

If you are buying a ticket in a Spanish-speaking country, the word you use may vary from one country to another. Here are some examples.

billete	Spain and many other Spanish speaking areas.
boleto	Argentina, Cuba, Chile, Mexico, Panama, Peru, Puerto Rico, Venezuela
pasaje	Argentina, Costa Rica, Dominican Republic
tiquete	Colombia
ticket	Dominican Republic, Venezuela

180. Can I go on the standby list?
¿Puede ponerme en la lista de espera? *PWEH-deh poh-NEHR-meh ehn lah LEES-tah deh ehs-PEHR-ah?*

181. What time does the _____leave (arrive)?
¿A qué hora sale (llega) el _____?
ah keh OH-rah SAH-leh (YEH-gah) ehl _____?

Baggage/El Equipaje

182. Baggage. El equipaje. *ehl eh-kee-PAH-heh.*

183. Suitcase. La maleta. *lah mah-LEH-tah.*

184. I want to leave these bags for a while.
Quiero dejar estas maletas un rato. *kee-EH-roh DEH-hahr EHS-tahs mah-LEH-tahs oon RAH-toh.*

24

If you need the services of a porter, ask for a *maletero* unless you are in Colombia or Cuba, where the word is *portero*. In Spain the porter would be *el mozo*, while in Venezuela you would ask for a *cargador de maletas*.

185. Where is the baggage room?
¿Dónde se factura el equipaje?
DOHN-deh seh fahk-TOOR-ah ehl eh-kee-PAH-heh?

186. Do I pay now or later?
¿Debo pagar ahora o después?
DEH-boh pah-GAHR ah-OH-rah oh dehs-PWEHS?

187. I want to take out my baggage.
Quiero reclamar mi equipaje.
kee-EH-roh reh-klah-MAHR mee-eh-kee-PAH-heh.

188. That is mine over there. Aquél es el mío.
ah-KEHL ehs ehl MEE-oh.

189. Handle this very carefully. Mucho cuidado con esto.
MOO-choh kwee-DAH-doh kohn EHS-toh.

Train/El Tren

190. I am going by train to _____.
Voy en tren a _____. *boy ehn trehn ah _____.*

191. Is it a direct (express, local) train?
¿Es un tren directo (expreso, local)? *ehs oon trehn dee-REHK-toh (ehks-preh-soh, loh-KAHL)?*

25

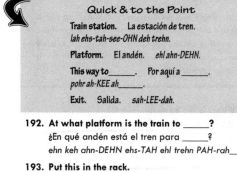

Quick & to the Point

Train station. La estación de tren.
lah ehs-tah-see-OHN deh trehn.

Platform. El andén. *ehl ahn-DEHN.*

This way to_____. Por aquí a _____.
pohr ah-KEE ah_____.

Exit. Salida. *sah-LEE-dah.*

192. **At what platform is the train to _____?**
¿En qué andén está el tren para _____?
ehn keh ahn-DEHN ehs-TAH ehl trehn PAH-rah_____?

193. **Put this in the rack.**
Ponga esto en el portaequipaje.
POHN-gah EHS-toh ehn ehl pohr-tah-eh-kee-PAH-heh.

194. **Is the train for _____ on time?**
¿Está a tiempo el tren para _____?
ehs-TAH ah tee-EHM-poh ehl trehn PAH-rah _____?

195. **It is ten minutes late.** Está retrasado diez minutos.
eh-STAH reh-trah-SAH-doh dee-EHS mee-NOO-tohs.

196. **Do I have to change trains?**
¿Necesito cambiar de tren?
neh-seh-SEE-toh kahm-bee-AHR deh trehn?

197. **Ticket collector.** Revisor (revisora).
reh-bee-SOHR (reh-bee-SOH-rah)

198. **Do you mind if I put the window down (up)?**
¿Le importa si bajo (subo) la ventana?
leh eem-POHR-tah see BAH-hoh (SOO-boh) lah behn-TAH-nah?

26

199. Please close (open) the window.
Por favor cierre (abra) la ventanilla.   *pohr fah-BOHR see-EH-rreh (AH-brah) lah behn-tah-NEE-yah.*

200. Where is the dining room (smoker)?
¿Dónde está el comedor (el carro fumador)?
DOH-deh ehs-TAH ehl koh-meh-DOHR (ehl KAH-rroh foo-mah-DOHR)?

201. Do you mind my smoking? ¿Le molesta que fume?
leh moh-LEHS-tah keh FOO-meh?

202. Can you give me a match?
¿Puede usted darme un fósforo?
PWEH-deh oos-TEHD DAHR-me oon FOHS-foh-roh?

203. What time is breakfast?
¿A qué hora sirven el desayuno?
ah keh OH-rah SEER-vehn ehl deh-sah-YOO-noh?

204. Excuse me. (when making your way to the door.)
Perdón.   *pehr-DOHN.*

205. Sleeping car. Coche cama.   *KOH-cheh KAH-mah.*

Spain's national railway is called RENFE and it is quick and efficient. It is also called Talgo, Expreso, and Rápido. They also have the AVE, which stands for Alta Velocidad Española (Spanish High Speed), which is the world's fastest train in commercial use. On one of its routes it travels 621 km. (386 mi.) between two cities in 2 hours and 38 minutes!

206. Dining car. Vagón restaurante.
bah-GOHN reh-stahw-RAHN-teh.

Bus/El Autobús

207. How often do the buses go to _____?
¿Con qué frecuencia salen los autobuses a _____?
kohn keh freh-KWEN-see-ah SAH-lehn lohs ahw-toh-
BOO-sehs ah _____?

Quick & to the Point

Ticket. El billete, el pasaje.
ehl bee-YEH-teh, el pah-SAH-heh

Where is the ticket office? ¿Dónde está la taquilla?
DOHN-deh ehs-TAH lah tah-KEE-yah?

Where can I buy a ticket? ¿Dónde puedo comprar el billete?
DOHN-deh PWEH-doh kohm-PRAHR ehl bee-YEH-teh?

Do you have a timetable? ¿Tiene un horario?
tee-EH-neh oon oh-RAH-ree-oh?

Does this bus go to _____? ¿Va este autobús a _____?
bah EHS-teh ahw-toh-BOOS ah_____?

When can I get on the bus?
¿Cuándo puedo subir al autobús?
KWAHN-doh PWEH-doh soo-BEER ahl ahw-toh-BOOS?

I want to get off the bus. Quiero bajarme del autobús.
kee-EH-roh bah-HAHR-meh dehl ahw-toh-BOOS.

208. Where is the bus/tram stop?

¿Dónde está la parada de autobús/tranvía?

DOHN-deh ehs-TAH lah pah-RAH-dah deh ahw-toh-BOOS/trahn-VEE-ah?

209. How much is the fare?

¿Cuánto cuesta el pasaje?

KWAH-toh KWEHS-tah ehl pah-SAH-heh?

210. A transfer please.   Un transbordo, por favor.

oon trahns-BOHR-doh, pohr fah-BOHR.

211. Which bus goes to_____?

¿Qué autobús va a _____?

keh ahw-toh-BOOS bah ah _____?

212. One ticket, please.   Un billete, por favor.

oon bee-YEH-teh, pohr fah-BOHR.

213. Can I buy an excursion ticket?

¿Puedo comprar un billete de excursión?

PWEH-doh kohm-PRAHR oon bee-YEH-teh deh ehks-koor-see-OHN?

214. Is there a stop for lunch?   ¿Paran para comer?

PAH-rahn PAH-rah koh-MEHR?

215. Can you stop over on the way?

¿Se puede hacer escalas en el camino?

seh PWEH-deh ah-SEHR ehs-KAH-lahs ehn ehl kah-MEE-noh?

216. Could you let me know when we get to _____?

¿Puede avisarme cuando lleguemos a _____?

PWEH-deh ah-bee-SAHR-meh KWAN-doh yeh-GEH-mohs ah_____?

217. The next stop. La próxima parada.
lah PROHK-see-mah pah-RAH-dah.

218. Two more blocks. Dos cuadras más.
dohs KWAH-drahs mahs.

219. Please tell me where to get off.
Por favor, avíseme dónde me bajo.
pohr fah-BOHR ah-BEE-seh-meh DOHN-deh meh
BAH-hoh.

Buses/Autobuses

Autobús is the generally accepted word for bus, but many other words are used throughout the Spanish-speaking world. The term sometimes varies from one part of the country to another.

bus	Spain, Argentina, Colombia, Costa Rica, Panama
buseta	Colombia
guagua	Cuba, Puerto Rico, Dominican Republic
ómnibus	Peru, Uruguay
camión	Mexico
camioneta	Guatemala, El Salvador
colectivo	Argentina, Bolivia, Colombia
grande buseta	larger buses in Colombia
el micro	Chile
lata	Costa Rica
carro	informally in Mexico

Boat/El Barco

220. Cruise ship.   El barco de cruceros.
ehl BAHR-koh deh kroo-CEHR-ohs.

221. What time do we board?
¿A qué hora hacemos bordo?
ah keh OHR-ah ah-SEH-mohs BOHR-doh?

222. I need something for seasickness.
Necesito algo para el mareo.
nehs-eh-SEE-toh AHL-goh PAH-rah ehl mah-REH-oh.

223. Can one go by boat to _____?
¿Se puede ir por barco a _____?
seh PWEH-deh eer pohr BAHR-koh ah _____?

224. When does the next boat leave?
¿Cuándo sale el próximo barco?   *KWAHN-doh*
SAH-leh ehl PROHK-see-moh BAHR-koh?

225. When must I go on board?
¿A qué hora debo embarcar?
ah keh OH-rah DEH-boh ehm-bahr-KAHR?

226. Can I land at _____?
¿Puedo desembarcar en _____?
PWEH-doh dehs-ehm-bahr-KAHR ehn_____?

227. Are meals served on the boat?
¿Se sirven comidas a bordo?
seh SEER-vehn koh-MEE-dahs ah BOHR-doh?

228. The captain, the purser.
El capitán, el contador.
ehl kah-pee-TAHN, ehl kohn-tah-DOHR.

31

229. The steward, on deck.

El mayordomo, sobre cubierta.

ehl mah-yohr-DOH-moh, SOH-breh koo-bee-EHR-tah.

230. I want to rent a deck chair.

Quiero alquilar una silla.

kee-EH-roh ahl-kee-LAHR OOH-nah SEE-yah.

231. I am a little seasick.

Estoy un poco mareado.

ehs-TOY oon POH-koh mah-reh-AH-doh.

232. I am going to my cabin.

Voy a mi camarote.   *boy ah mee kah-mah-ROH-teh.*

233. Let's go to the dining salon (the bar).

Vamos al comedor (al bar or a la cantina).

BAH-mohs ahl koh-meh-DOHR (ahl bahr or ah lah kahn-TEE-nah).

Rock the boat. While on board the ship you will have plenty of time to practice communicating skills. Don't be shy. Use the phrases you have, but also use your other communication skills. You could ask for an egg by using the word for egg or clucking like a hen or showing shape. Smiles are universal. The first skill you need to communicate in another language is the willingness to try. Be dramatic and use educated guesses to communicate. Don't worry about making mistakes. Go ahead and try. It will be fun!

234. A lifeboat, a life preserver.

Una lancha, un salvavidas.

OO-nah LAHN-chah, oon sahl-bah-BEE-dahs.

Bicycles/Bicicletas

235. Can you recommend a good place for a bike ride?

¿Me puede recomendar algún sitio bonito para pasear en bicicleta? *meh PWEH-deh reh-koh-mehn-DAHR ahl-GOON see-TEE-oh boh-NEE-toh PAH-rah pah-seh-AHR ehn bee-see-KLEH-tah?*

236. Is it within cycling distance?

¿Está a distancia de bicicleta? *ehs-TAH ah dees-tahn-SEE-ah deh-bee-see-CLEH-tah?*

237. Is it safe to cycle around here?

¿Es seguro montar bicicleta aquí? *ehs seh-GOO-roh MOHN-tahr bee-see-KLEH-tah ah-KEE?*

238. Where can I rent bicycles?

¿Dónde se aquilan bicicletas? *DOHN-deh seh ahl-KEE-lahn bee-see-KLEH-tahs?*

239. How much to rent a bicycle for an hour (morning/ afternoon/day)?

¿Cuánto vale alquilar una bicicleta durante una hora (toda la mañana/la tarde/un día)? *KWAHN-toh BAH-leh ahl-kee-LAHR OO-nah bee-see-KLEH-tah doo-RAHN-teh OO-nah OH-rah (TOH-dah lah mah-NYA-nah/lah TAHR-deh/oon DEE-ah)?*

240. Can you lend me a padlock?
¿Me puede prestar un candado?
meh PWEH-deh PREHS-tahr oon-kahn-DAH-doh?

241. Can you raise (lower) the seat?
¿Me puede subir (bajar) el sillín?
meh PWEH-deh soo-BEER (bah-HAHR) ehl see-YEEN?

242. Do I have to wear a helmet?
¿Es obligatorio llevar casco?
ehs oh-blee-gah-TOH-ree-oh yeh-BAHR KAHS-koh?

243. Where can I park the bike?
¿Dónde puedo aparcar la bicicleta?   *DOHN-deh PWEH-doh ah-pahr-KAHR lah bee-see-KLEH-tah?*

244. Where are repairs done?
¿Dónde arreglan bicicletas?
DOHN-deh ah-RREH-glahn bee-see-KLEH-tahs?

245. I have a flat tire.   Se me ha pinchado una rueda.
seh meh ah peen-CHAH-doh OO-nah roo-EH-dah.

246. I fell off of my bike.   Me he caído de la bici.
meh eh kah-EE-doh deh lah BEE-see.

247. Bike.   La bici, la bicicleta.   *lah BEE-see, lah bee-see-KLEH-tah.*

248. Breaks.   Los frenos.   *lohs freh-nohs.*

249. To cycle.   Montar (andar) en bicicleta.
mohn-TAHR (ahn-DAHR) ehn bee-see-KLEH-tah.

250. Gear shift.   El cambio de marchas.
ehl kahm-BEE-oh deh MAR-chahs.

251. Handlebars.   El manillar.   *ehl mah-nee-YAHR.*

Animal Sounds in Spanish

Bicycling through the countryside give you a great close-up view of the farms (las granjas) and houses. You can enjoy the sights and sounds all around you. In case you need interpretation for the Spanish farm and zoo animals, we've included a list of Spanish animal sounds!

Owl	Búho	*uu uu*
Donkey	Burro	*iii-aah*
Horse	Caballo	*jiiiiii*
Goat	Cabra	*bee bee*
Pig	Cerdo	*oink-oink*
Hen	Gallina	*kara-kara-kara*
Rooster	Gallo	*ki-ki-ri-ki*
Cat	Gato	*meow*
Lion	León	*grrr, grgrgr*
Sheep	Oveja	*bee, mee*
Monkey	Mono	*i-i-i*
Duck	Pato	*cuac cuac*
Dog	Perro	*guau guau guau*
Chick	Pollito	*pío, pío*
Frog	Rana	*cruá cruá or berp berp*
Tiger	Tigre	*gr-gr-gr*
Cow	Vaca	*muuuu*

252. Helmet. El casco. *ehl KAHS-koh.*

253. Inner tube. La cámara. *lah KAHM-ah-rah.*

254. Lights. Las luces. *lahs LOO-sehs.*

255. Mountain bike. La bicicleta de montaña.
lah bee-see-KLEH-tah deh mohn-TAH-nyah.

256. Racing bike. La bicicleta de carreras.
lah bee-see-KLEH-tah de kah-RREH-rrahs.

257. Tandem. El tándem. *ehl TAHN-dehm.*

258. Padlock. El candado. *ehl kahn-DAH-doh.*

259. Wheel. La rueda. *lah roo-EH-dah.*

260. Puncture. El pinchazo. *ehl peen-CHAH-soh.*

261. Pump. La bomba. *lah BOHM-bah.*

262. Seat (saddle). El sillín. *ehl see-YEEN.*

263. Tire. La rueda. *lah roo-EH-dah.*

Metro/El Metro

264. Subway entrance. La entrada al metro.
lah ehn-TRAH-dah ahl MEH-troh.

265. Subway exit. La salida de metro.
lah sah-LEE-dah deh MEH-troh.

266. Subway station. La estación de metro.
lah eh-stah-see-OHN deh MEH-troh.

267. Which line do I take to _____?
¿Qué línea cojo (tomo) para_____? *keh LEE-neh-ah
COH-hoh (TOH-moh) PAH-rah _____?*

268. What is the next station?
¿Cuál es la próxima estación?
kwahl ehs lah PROHK-see-mah ehs-tah-see-OHN?

269. This way to _____ exit. Por aquí a _____ salida.
pohr ah-KEE ah _____ sah-LEE-dah.

270. Change (coins). El cambio. *ehl KAHM-bee-oh.*

271. Destination. El destino. *ehl dehs-TEE-noh.*

272. Line. La línea. *lah LEE-neh-ah.*

273. Ticket machine. La venta automática de billetes.
lah BEHN-tah ahw-toh-MAH-tee-kah deh bee-YEH-tehs.

274. Leave me alone! ¡Déjame en paz!
DEH-hah-meh ehn pahs!

275. Help, thief! ¡Socorro, ladrón!
soh-KOH-rroh! lah-DROHN!

Mexico's metro is a tourist destination in itself. If you take line 3 to the Pino Suárez station, you will find an Aztec pyramid discovered in 1968 during the construction of the Metro line. Or take line 4 to Talismán station and see the remains of a mammoth that is more than thirteen thousand years old. Or take line 2 to the very entertaining Chapultepec Park. The metro is modern, clean, safe, cheap, and efficient.

Taxi/ El Taxi

276. Please call me a taxi. Por favor, llámeme un taxi.
poh fah-BOHR, yah-MEH-meh oon TAHK-see.

277. Are you free? ¿Está libre? *ehs-TAH LEE-breh?*

278. Please take me to this address.
Por favor, lléveme a esta dirección. *pohr fah-
BOHR YEH-beh-meh ah EHS-tah dee-rrek-see-OHN.*

279. How far is it? ¿A qué distancia está?
ah keh dees-TAHN-see-ah ehs-TAH?

280. How much will it cost? ¿Cuánto costaría?
KWAHN-toh kohs-tah-REE-ah?

281. That's too much. Eso es demasiado.
EH-soh ehs deh-mah-see-AH-doh.

282. How much is it to go to _____?
¿Cuánto cuesta (vale) ir a _____?
KWAHN-toh KWEHS-tah (BAH-leh) eer ah _____?

Quick & to the Point

How much to the . . . ? ¿Cuánto cuesta ir a . . . ?
KWAHN-toh KWEHS-tah eer ah. . . ?

. . . to this address? . . . a esta dirección?
ah EHS-tah dee-rehk-see-OHN?

. . . to the airport? . . . al aeropuerto? *ahl ah-reh-oh-
PWEHR-toh?*

. . . downtown? . . . al centro de la ciudad?
ahl SEHN-troh deh lah see-oo-DAHD?

283. Does that include luggage?
¿El precio incluye el equipaje?
ehl PREH-see-oh een-CLOO-yeh ehl eh kee-PAH-heh?

284. Please slow down. Por favor, vaya más despacio.
pohr fah-BOHR VAH-yah mahs dehs-PAH-see-oh.

285. Please hurry. Por favor, de prisa.
pohr fah-BOHR, deh PREE-sah.

286. The next corner, please.
La próxima esquina, por favor.
lah PROK-see-mah ehs-KEE-nah, pohr fah-BOHR.

287. Stop here. Wait for me. Pare aquí. Espéreme.
PAH-reh ah-KEE. ehs-PEH-reh-meh.

288. Go by way of _____. Vaya por _____.
VAH-yah pohr _____.

Taxis in Spain are cheap, except to and from the airport. (In Madrid, you can take an inexpensive metro ride to and from the airport.) Taxis usually hold up to four people. A taxi stand is called a *parada de taxi.* You can let the driver know where you want to go by stating your destination, plus "please." *La Plaza Mayor, por favor.* Carrying a card with the address of your hotel will also help you give the driver your correct destination.

289. How much do I owe you? ¿Cuánto le debo?
KWAHN-toh leh DEH-boh?

Streetcar and Local Bus/*El Tranvia y El Autobús*

In smaller towns, buses may be cheaper and faster than trains. Bus schedules are usually available at tourist offices.

290. Which stop for _____? ¿Qué parada para _____?
keh pah-RAH-dah PAHR-ah._____?

291. Tell me when to get off.
Dígame cuándo tengo que bajarme.
DEE-gah-meh KWAHN-doh TEHN-go keh bah-HAHR-meh.

292. The bus stop. La parada de autobús.
lah pah-RAH-dah deh ahw-toh-BOOS.

293. The conductor, driver. El conductor, el chofer.
ehl kohn-dook-TOHR, ehl choh-FEHR.

294. What bus (streetcar) do I take for _____?
¿Qué autobús (tranvía) tomo para _____?
keh ahw-toh-BOOS (trahn-BEE-ah) TOH-moh PAH-rah _____?

295. Where does the bus for _____ stop?
¿Dónde para el bus para _____?
DOHN-deh PAH-rah ehl boos PAH-rah _____?

296. Do you go near _____? ¿Pasa cerca de _____?
PAH-sah SEHR-kah deh _____?

297. How much is the fare?
¿Cuánto cuesta el pasaje?
KWAHN-toh KWEHS-tah el pah-SAH-heh?

298. A transfer, please. Un transbordo, por favor.
oon trahns-BOHR-doh, por fah-BOHR.

299. The next stop. La próxima parada.
lah PROHK-see-mah pah-RAH-dah.

300. Two blocks away. Dos cuadras más.
dohs KWAH-drahs mahs.

Automobiles/Los Automóviles

301. Where is there a gas station (a garage)?
¿Dónde hay una gasolinera (un garaje or taller)?
DOHN-deh i-oo-nah gah-soh-lee-NEH-rah (oon gah-RAH-hey or tah-YEHR)?

Quick & to the Point

Car. El coche. *ehl koh-cheh.*

Gas. La gasolina. *lah gah-soh-LEE-nah.*

Gas station. La gasolinera. *lah gah-soh-lee-NEH-rah.*

Where can I park? ¿Dónde puedo estacionar?
DOHN-deh pweh-doh ehs-tah-see-oh-NAHR?

Parking lot. El estacionamiento.
ehl ehs-tah-see-oh-nah-mee-EHN-toh.

Speed limit. Velocidad máxima.
beh-loh-see-DAHD MAHK-see-mah.

Stop. Pare. *PAH-reh.*

302. How much is gas per liter?

¿Cuánto cuesta la gasolina por litro?   *KWAHN-toh KWEHS-tah lah gah-soh-LEE-nah pohr LEE-troh.*

303. Give me _____liters of gasoline.

Déme _____ litros de gasolina.
DEH-meh _____LEE-trohs de gah-soh-LEE-nah.

304. Please fill the tank.

Por favor, lléne el tanque de gas.
pohr fah-BOHR, YEH-neh ehl TAHN-keh deh gahs.

305. Please check the oil, water, and air.

Por favor, revise el nivel del aceite, del agua y el aire.   *pohr fah-BOHR, reh-BEE-seh ehl nee-BEHL dehl ah-SAY-teh, dehl AH-gwah ee ehl I-reh.*

306. Please change the oil.   Por favor, cambie el aceite.
pohr-fah-BOHR, KAHM-bee-eh ehl ah-SAY-teh.

307. Put water in the battery.

Ponga agua en la batería.
POHN-gah AH-gwah en lah bah-teh-REE-ah.

308. Can you recommend a mechanic?

¿Quiere recomendarme un mecánico?   *kee-EH-reh re- koh-mehn-DAHR-meh oon meh-KAH-nee-koh?*

309. I have an international driver's license.

Tengo un carnet de conducir internacional.
TEHN-go oon kahr-NEHT deh kon-doo-SEER een-tehr-nah-see-oh-NAHL.

310. What is this (the next) town?

¿Cómo se llama este (el próximo) pueblo?

KOH-moh seh YA-mah EHS-teh (ehl PROK-see-moh) PWEH-bloh?

311. Where can I rent a car?

¿Dónde puedo alquilar un coche?

DOHN-deh PWEH-doh ahl-KEE-lahr oon KOH-cheh?

312. How much is it per day (week)?

¿Cuánto cuesta por día (por semana)? *KWAN-toh KWEHS-tah pohr DEE-ah (pohr seh-MAH-nah)?*

313. Does that include insurance (mileage)?

¿Incluye el seguro (el millaje)?

een-klooh-yeh ehl seh-GOO-roh (ehl mee-yah-heh)?

Words to help you in finding your way.

city map. el mapa de la ciudad.
ehl MAH-pah deh lah see-oo-DAHD.
road map. el mapa de carretera.
ehl MAH-pah deh kah-reh-TEH-rah.
left. izquierda. *ees-kee-EHR-dah.*
right. derecha. *deh-REH-chah.*
straight ahead. todo derecho.
TOH-doh deh-REH-choh.
first. primero. *pree-MEHR-oh.*
next. siguiente. *see-gee-EHN-teh.*
corner. la esquina. *lah ehs-KEE-nah.*

43

314. How long can I park here?

¿Cuánto tiempo puedo aparcar aquí?   *KWAN-toh tee-EHM-poh PWEH-do ah-pahr-CAHR ah-KEE?*

Help on the Road/ La Ayuda en la Carretera

315. My car has broken down.
Mi coche no funciona.
mee KOH-cheh noh foon-see-OH-nah.

316. Can you tow (push) me?
¿Puede usted remolcarme (empujarme)?   *PWEH-de oos-TEHD reh-mohl-KAHR-meh (ehm-poo-HAHR-meh)?*

317. Will you put on the spare?
¿Quiere usted poner la rueda de repuesto?
kee-EHR-eh oos-TEHD poh-NEHR lah roo-EH-dah de re- PWEHS-toh?

Quick & to the Point
Car Trouble

Accident. El accidente. *ehl ahk-see-DEHN-teh.*

Breakdown. El averiado. *ehl ah-beh-ree-AH-doh.*

Flat tire. La rueda pinchada. *lah roo-EH-dah peen-CHAH-dah.*

Dead battery. La batería descargada.
lah bah-teh-REE-ah dehs-kahr-GAH-dah.

We need a tow truck. Necesitamos una grúa.
neh-sehs-ee-TAH-mohs OO-nah GROO-ah.

318. Will you take me to a garage?
¿Quiere usted llevarme a un garaje? *kee-EH-reh oos-TEHD yeh-BAHR-meh ah oon gah-RAH-heh?*

319. The battery is dead. La batería no funciona.
lah bah-teh-REE-ah noh foon-see-OH-nah.

320. I have a flat tire. Tengo un pinchazo.
TEHN-goh oon peen-CHAH-soh.

321. I've lost my car keys.
He perdido las llaves de mi coche.
eh pehr-DEE-doh lahs YAH-behs deh mee KOH-cheh.

322. I've run out of gas. Me he quedado sin gasolina.
meh eh keh-DAH-doh seen-gah-soh-LEE-nah.

323. Change the tire. Cambie esta llanta.
KAM-bee-eh EHS-tah YAHN-tah.

324. The engine overheats. El motor se calienta.
ehl MOH-tohr seh kah-lee-EHN-tah.

325. The _____ doesn't work (well).
_____ no funciona (bien).
_____ noh foon-see-OH-nah (bee-EHN).

326. Toll road. Autopista. *ahw-toh-PEES-tah.*

Gas prices in Spain are per liter, and there are about 4 liters per gallon.

Parts of a Car/Las Partes del Coche

327. Battery, brakes, clutch. la batería, los frenos, el embrague. *lah bah-teh-REE-ah, lohs FREH-nohs, ehl ehm-BRAH-geh.*

328. Driver's license. El carnet, el permiso de conducir. *ehl kahr-NEHT, ehl pehr-MEE-soh deh kohn-doo-SEER.*

329. Engine, accelerator.
El motor, el acelerador. *ehl moh-TOHR, ehl ahk-seh-leh-rah-DOHR.*

330. Steering wheel, spare tire.
El volante, la rueda de repuesto. *ehl boh-LAHN-teh, lah roo-EH-dah deh reh-PWEHS-toh.*

331. Headlights, taillights.
Los faros, los faros traseros. *lohs FAH-rohs, lohs FAH-rohs trah-SEH-rohs.*

332. Radiator, windshield. El radiador, el parabrisas. *ehl rah-dee-ah-DOHR, ehl pah-rah-BREES-sahs.*

Quick & to the Point

hood. el capo. *ehl CAH-poh.*

trunk. el baúl. *ehl bah-OOL.*

horn. el claxon. *ehl CLAHK-sohn.*

seatbelt. el cinturón de seguridad.
ehl seen-too-ROHN deh seh-goor-ee-DAHD.

license plate. la placa. *lah PLAH-kah.*

keys. las llaves. *lahs YAH-behs.*

When traveling in Spanish-speaking countries, you will see signs for "gasolinera" and "taller." A "taller" also means *garage* and has a workshop to service cars. It may also sell gas. A "gasolinera" generally just sells gas.

333. **Seatbelt.** El cinturón de seguridad.
     ehl seen-toor-ROHN deh seh-goo-ree-DAHD.

Tools and Equipment/*Las Herramientas y el Equipo*

334. **Nail.** El clavo. *ehl CLAH-boh.*

335. **Toolbox.** La caja de herramientas.
     lah CAH-jah deh ehrr-ah-mee-EHN-tahs.

336. **Chains.** Las cadenas. *lahs kah-DEH-nahs.*

337. **Hammer.** El martillo. *ehl mahr-TEE-yoh.*

338. **Jack.** El gato. *ehl GAH-toh.*

339. **Key.** La llave. *lah YAH-beh.*

340. **Pliers.** Las pinzas. *lahs PEEN-sahs.*

341. **Rope.** Una cuerda. *OO-nah KWER-dah.*

342. **Screwdriver.** El destornillador.
     ehl dehs-tohr-nee-yah-DOR.

343. **Tire pump.** La bomba de neumáticos.
     lah BOHM-bah deh neh-oo-MAH-tee-kohs.

344. Monkey wrench, bolt.   La llave inglesa, el tornillo.
lah YAH-beh een-GLEH-sah, ehl tohr-NEE-yoh.

Road Signs and Public Notices/*Los Letreros del Camino y los Rótulos Públicos*

345. Stop ahead.   Parada más adelante.
pah-RAH-dah mahs ah-deh-LAHN-teh.

346. Speed limit.   Límite de velocidad.
LEE-mee-teh deh beh-loh-see-DAHD.

347. Yield.   Ceda el paso.   *SEH-dah ehl PAH-soh.*

348. Detour.   Desvío.   *dehs-BEE-oh.*

Quick & to the Point

Pedestrian crossing.   Cruce /Paseo de peatones.
kroo-seh/ pah-SEH-oh deh peh-ah-TOH-nehs.

Walk.   Camine.   *kah-MEE-neh.*

Do not cross.   No cruzar.   *noh kroo-SAHR.*

No smoking.   No fumar.   *noh foo-MAHR.*

Closed.   Cerrado.   *seh-RRAH-doh.*

Open.   Abierto.   *ah-bee-EHR-toh.*

Stop.   Pare/Alto.   *PAH-reh/ AHL-toh.*

Exit.   Salida.   *sah-LEE-dah.*

Entrance.   Entrada.   *ehn-TRAH-dah.*

For rent.   Se alquila.   *seh alh-KEE-lah.*

For sale.   Se vende.   *seh BEHN-deh.*

349. No entry. No entre. *noh EHN-treh.*

350. Slow. Despacio. *dehs-PAH-see-oh.*

351. Slow down. Frene. *FREH-neh.*

352. No passing. No adelantar/no pasar. *noh ah-deh-lahn-TAHR/noh pah-SAHR.*

353. Work area. Obras. *OH-brahs.*

354. School zone. Zona escolar. *SOH-nah ehs-coh-LAHR.*

355. Railroad crossing. F.C. (ferrocarril). *efe seh (feh-rroh-kah-RREEL).*

356. Keep clear. Vado permanente. *BAH-doh pehr-mah-NEHN-teh.*

357. Danger. Peligro/precaución. *peh-LEE-groh/preh-caw-see-OHN.*

358. Caution. Precaución. *preh-caw-see-OHN.*

359. Keep out. Prohibido el paso. *proh-ee-BEE-doh ehl PAH-soh.*

360. One way. Sentido único. *sehn-TEE-doh OON-ee-koh*

361. Wrong way. Vía equivocada. *BEE-ah eh-kee-boh-KAH-dah.*

362. Speed bump. Tope, badén. *TOH-peh, bah-DEHN.*

363. Toll. Peaje, cobro. *peh-AH-heh, KOH-broh.*

364. Parking. Estacionamiento. *ehs-tah-see-oh-nah-mee-EHN-toh.*

365. No Parking. Prohibido estacionar.
proh-ee-BEE-doh ehs tah-see-oh-NAHR.

366. Emergency. Emergencia. *eh-mehr-hehn-SEE-ah.*

367. Curve. Curva. *KOOR-bah.*

368. Traffic circle. Glorieta. *gloh-ree-EH-tah.*

369. Restrooms. Sanitarios/aseos.
Sah-nee-TAH-ree-ohs/ ah-SEH-ohs.

370. Men. Caballeros/Señores.
kah-bah-YEH-rohs/seh-NYOH-rehs.

371. Ladies. Damas/Señoras/Mujeres.
DAH-mahs/seh-NYOH-rahs/moo-HEH-rehs.

Stop Signs

In Spanish-speaking countries you will be able to "read" a lot of the traffic signs because they use many of the shapes and symbols that we use. A stop sign will most likely be red and shaped like the ones familiar to us. It could have several different words on it. It may read:

ALTO which is used throughout the Spanish-speaking world

PARE in Argentina, Chile, Colombia, or Puerto Rico

STOP in Spain!

---

372. Out of order.   Descompuesto, fuera de servicio.
dehs-kohm-PWEHS-toh, foo-EH-rah deh
sehr-BEE-see-oh.

373. Do not litter.   No tire basura.
noh TEE-reh bah-SOO-rah.

374. Street, avenue, boulevard.   Calle, avenida, bulevar.
KAH-yeh, ah-beh-NEE-dah, boo-leh-BAHR.

Lodging/*El Alojamiento*

The Hotel and Inn/*El Hotel y la Posada*

375. Which hotel is good (inexpensive)?
¿Cuál de los hoteles es bueno (barato)?   *kwahl deh*
lohs oh-TEH-lehs ehs BWEH-noh (bah-RAH-toh)?

376. The best hotel.   El mejor hotel.
ehl meh-HOHR oh-TEHL.

377. Not too expensive.   No muy caro.
noh moo-ee KAH-roh.

378. I (don't) want to be in the center of town.
(No) quiero estar en el centro.
(noh) kee-EH-roh ehs-TAHR ehn ehl SEHN-troh.

379. Where it is not too noisy.   Dónde no haya ruido.
DOHN-deh noh I-yah roo-EE-doh.

380. On what floor?   ¿En qué piso?   *ehn keh PEE-soh?*

381. Is there an elevator?   ¿Hay ascensor?
i ah-sehn-SOHR?

Quick & to the Point

Do you have a room? ¿Tiene una habitación?
tee-EH-neh OO-nah ah-bee-tah-see-OHN?

I would like a private bath. Me gustaría un baño privado.
meh goos-tah-REE-ah oon BAH-nyoh pree-VAH-doh.

How much does it cost? ¿Cuánto cuesta?
KWAHN-toh KWEHS-tah?

Can I use a credit card?
¿Puedo usar una tarjeta de crédito?
PWEH-doh oo-SAHR OO-nah tahr-HEH-tah deh KREH-dee-toh?

What time is check-out?
¿A qué hora tenemos que dejar el hotel?
ah keh OHR-ah teh-NEH-mohs keh deh-HAHR ehl oh-TEHL?

Is breakfast included? ¿El desayuno está incluido?
ehl dehs-ah-YOO-noh ehs-TAH een-kloo-EE-doh?

Does the room have an air conditioner?
¿Tiene la habitación aire acondicionado?
tee-EH-neh lah ah-bee-tah-see-OHN I-reh ah-kohn-dee-see-oh-NAH-doh?

Elevator. Ascensor. *ah-sehn-SOHR.*

382. Do you have any rooms available?
¿Tiene habitaciones libres?
tee-EH-neh ah-bee-tah-see-OH-nehs LEE-brehs?

383. For three nights. Para tres noches.
PAH-rah trehs NOH-chehs.

384. How much per night (person)?

¿Cuánto cuesta por noche (por persona)?

KWAHN-toh KWEHS-tah pohr NOH-cheh (pohr pehr-SOH-nah)?

385. Is there a student (children, senior citizen) discount?

¿Hay un descuento para estudiantes (niños, jubilados)?

i oon dehs-KWEHN-toh PAH-rah ehs-too-dee-AHN-tehs (NEE-nyohs, joo-bee-LAH-dohs)?

386. I have a reservation for _____.

Tengo reservado para_____.

TEHN-goh reh-sehr-VAH-doh pah-rah_____.

387. I want to make a reservation for _____.

Quiero reservar _____.

kee-EH-roh reh-sehr-BAHR _____

388. I want a room with (without) meals.

Quiero un cuarto con (sin) comidas.   *kee-EH-roh oon KWAHR-toh kohn (seen) koh-MEE-dahs.*

389. I want a single (double) room.

Quiero un cuarto para uno (para dos).   *kee-EH-roh oon KWAHR-toh PAH-rah OO-noh (PAH-rah dohs).*

390. A single.   Cuarto sencillo.

KWAHR-toh sehn-SEE-yoh.

391. A suite.   Una suite.   *oo-nah soo-EE-teh.*

392. With bath, shower, twin beds.

Con baño, ducha, camas gemelas.

kohn BAH-nyo, DOO-chah, KAH-mahs ge-MEH-lahs.

393. With double bed.   Con cama matrimonial.
Kohn kah-mah mah-tree-moh-nee-AHL.

394. A room with a window.   Un cuarto con ventana.
oon KWAHR-toh kohn behn TAH-nah.

395. In the front, at the back.   Al frente, al fondo.
ahl FREHN-teh, ahl FOHN-doh.

396. Upstairs, downstairs.   Arriba, abajo.
ah-RREE-bah, ah-BAH-hoh.

397. For tonight.   Por esta noche.
pohr EHS-tah NOH-cheh.

398. That's fine, I'll take it.   Vale, la alquilo.
BAH-leh, lah ahl-KEE-loh.

399. Can I pay by credit card?
¿Puedo pagar con tarjeta de crédito?   *PWEH-doh*
PAH-gahr kohn tahr-HEH-tah deh KREH-dee-toh?

400. Send me a bellman.   Mándeme un botones.
MAHN-dah-meh oon boh-TOH-nehs.

401. I want a room on a higher floor.
Quiero un cuarto en un piso más alto.   *kee-EH-roh*
oon KWAR-toh ehn oon PEE-soh mahs AHL-toh.

402. On a lower floor.   En un piso más bajo.
en oon PEE-soh mahs BAH-hoh.

403. I would like to see the room.
Quisiera ver el cuarto.
kee-see-EH-rah behr ehl KWAHR-toh.

404. Where is the bathroom? ¿Dónde está el baño?
DOHN-deh ehs-TAH ehl BAH-nyoh?

405. I (don't) like this one. Éste (no) me gusta.
EHS-teh (noh) meh GOOS-tah.

406. Do you have something better?
¿Tiene usted uno mejor?
tee-EH-neh oos-TEHD OO-noh meh-HOHR?

407. Cheaper, larger, something smaller.
Más barato, más grande, algo más pequeño.
*mahs bah-RAH-toh, mahs GRAHN-deh, AHL-goh
mahs peh-KEH-nyo.*

408. Please send _____ to my room.
Por favor mande _____ a mi cuarto.
pohr fah-BOHR MAHN-deh _____ ah mee KWAR-toh.

409. Date, date of birth. Fecha, fecha de nacimiento.
FEH-cha, FEH-cha deh nah-cee-mee-EHN-toh.

410. Name, surname, signature.
Nombre, apellido, firma.
NOHM-breh, ah-peh-YEE-doh, FEER-mah.

411. Could you wake me at _____?
¿Podría despertarme a las _____?
poh-DREE-ah dehs-pehr-TAHR-meh ah lahs _____?

412. Do not disturb me until _____.
No me moleste hasta _____.
noh meh moh-LEHS-teh AHS-tah _____.

413. Do you have a safe? ¿Tiene una caja fuerte?
tee-EH-neh OO-nah KAH-hah FWEHR-teh?

414. Can I leave this in the safe?
¿Puedo dejar esto en la caja fuerte? *PWEH-doh deh-HAHR ehs-toh ehn lah KAH-hah FWEHR-teh?*

415. Can I use the phone?
¿Puedo usar el teléfono? *PWEH-doh oo-SAHR-ehl teh-LEH-foh-noh?*

416. Is there an elevator? ¿Hay un ascensor? *I oon ah-sehn-SOHR?*

417. I've locked myself out of my room.
Cerré la puerta y se me olvidaron las llaves dentro. *seh-RREH lah PWEHR-tah ee seh meh ohl-bee-DAH-rohn lahs YAH-behs dehn-troh.*

418. Do you change money here?
¿Se cambia dinero en este hotel? *seh KAM-bee-ah dee-NEH-roh ehn EH-steh oh-TEHL?*

419. Should I leave my key at reception?
¿Tengo que dejar la llave en la recepcíon? *TEHN-goh keh deh-HAHR lah YAH-beh ehn lah reh-sehp-see-OHN?*

420. Can I leave a message? ¿Puedo dejar un mensaje? *PWEH-doh deh-HAHR oon mehn-SAH-heh?*

421. Are there any messages for me?
¿Hay algún mensaje para mí? *i ahl-GOON mehn-SAH-heh PAH-rah mee?*

422. I would like breakfast in my room.
Quisiera el desayuno en mi cuarto. *kee-see-EH-rah ehl deh-sah-YOO-noh ehn mee KWAR-toh.*

423. Could I have some laundry done?
   ¿Me pueden lavar la ropa?
   meh PWEH-dehn lah-BAHR lah ROH-pah?

424. I want some things pressed.
   Quiero tener planchados unos vestidos.   *kee-EH-roh
   teh-NEHR plahn-CHAH-dohs OO-nohs behs-TEE-dohs.*

425. The room needs to be cleaned.
   Hay que limpiar la habitación.   *i keh leem-pee-AHR
   lah ah-bee-tah-see-OHN.*

426. My room key, please.   Mi llave, por favor.
   mee YA-beh pohr fah-BOHR.

427. Please change the sheets.
   Por favor, cambie las sábanas.
   pohr fah-BOHR, KAHM-bee-eh lahs SAH-bah-nahs.

428. Do I have any letters or messages?
   ¿Hay cartas o mensajes para mí?
   i KAHR-tahs oh mehn-SAH-hehs PAH-rah mee?

429. When does the mail come?
   ¿A qué hora llega el correo?
   ah keh OH-rah YEH-gah ehl coh-RREH-oh?

430. What is my room number?
   ¿Cuál es el número de mi cuarto?
   kwahl ehs ehl NOO-meh-roh deh mee KWAR-toh?

431. I am leaving at _____ o'clock.   Salgo a las _____.
   SAHL-goh ah lahs _____.

432. I would like to speak to the manager.

Quisiera hablar con el gerente.

kee-see-EH-rah ah-BLAHR kohn ehl heh-REHN-teh.

433. Can baggage be stored here until _____?

¿Se puede guardar aquí el equipaje hasta _____?

seh PWEH-deh gwahr-DAHR a-KEE ehl eh-kee-PAH-heh AHS-tah _____?

Places to Stay

Besides hotels, there are many housing options for tourists. Many students and budget travelers save money by staying in youth hostels (albergue juvenil), which generally do not have many amenities and shared bathrooms, but are usually clean and widely available. Another option is to rent an apartment or home. For longer stays, this can be the best option, saving money on lodging while sometimes offering meals and/or cooking facilities. Smaller family-owned inns in the country ("pensión") may not offer all the facilities of a large chain hotel, but they can give you an authentic taste of the real culture. Check out the "paradores" in Spain. They are former estates and castles that have been turned into wonderful lodgings. Most have beautiful locations and often have great restaurants.

434. Can you give me an extra blanket? I'm cold.

¿Puede darme otra manta (cobija), por favor?
Tengo frío.

P WEH-deh DAHR-meh OH-trah MAHN-tah (koh-BEE-hah), pohr fah-BOHR? TEHN-goh FREE-oh.

In the Room/ En La Habitación

435. Can you show me how the televison works (remote control)?

¿Puede mostrarme cómo funciona la televisión (el control remoto)?

P WEH-deh mohs-TRAHR-meh KO-moh foon-SEE-oh-nah lah teh-leh bee-see-OHN (ehl kohn-TROHL reh-MOH-toh)?

Quick & to the Point

Room service. El servicio de habitación.
ehl sehr-BEE-cee-oh deh ah-bee-tah-see-OHN.

Ice bucket. El cubo de hielo. *ehl KOO-boh deh YEH-loh.*

Remote control. El control remoto.
ehl kohn-TROHL reh-MOH-toh.

Extra towels. Toallas extras. *toh-AH-yahs EHKS-trahs.*

Extra blanket. Manta extra. *MAHN-tah EHKS-trah.*

Extra pillow. Almohada extra. *ahl-moh-AH-dah EHKS-trah.*

Internet access. Acceso a internet.
ahk-SEH-soh ah een-tehr-NEHT.

Is Wi-Fi available in the room?
¿Está disponible wifi en la habitación?
ehs-TAH dees-poh-NEE-bleh WEE-fee ehn lah ah-bee-tah-see-OHN?

436. Is there Internet access here?
¿Hay acceso a la internet (la red) aquí? *i ahk-SEH-soh ah lah een-tehr-NEHT (lah rrehd) ah-KEE?*

437. May I have_____? ¿Puede darme _____?
PWEH-deh DAHR-meh _____?

438. Bath towel, pillow, hanger.
Una toalla de baño, una almohada, una percha.
OO-nah toh-AH-yah deh BAH-nyoh, OO-nah ahl-moh-AH-dah, OO-nah PEHR-chah.

439. Pillow case, bathmat. Una funda, un tapete de baño.
OO-nah FOON-dah, oon tah-PEH-teh deh BAH-nyoh.

440. Soap, shampoo, toothpaste.
El jabón, el champú, la pasta de dientes.
ehl hah-BOHN, ehl chahm-POO, lah PAHS-tah deh dee-EHN-tehs.

441. Drinking water, glass, toilet paper.
Agua para beber, el vaso, el papel higiénico.
AH-gwah PAH-rah beh-BEHR, ehl BAH-soh, ehl pah-PEHL ee-hee-EH-nee-koh.

442. Ice, ice water. El hielo, agua helada.
ehl YEH-loh, AH-gwah eh-LAH-dah.

443. Maid. La camarera. *lah kah-mah-REH-rah.*

444. The toilet won't flush.
La cadena del retrete no funciona. *lah cah-DEH-nah dehl reh-TREH-teh noh foon-see-OH-nah.*

445. The air conditioning doesn't work.
El aire acondicionado no funciona. *ehl AH-ee-reh ah-kon-dee-see-oh-NAH-doh noh foon-see-OH-nah.*

446. I can't open (close) the window.
No puedo abrir (cerrar) la ventana.   *noh PWEH-doh ah-BREER (seh-RRAHR) lah behn-TAH-nah.*

Signs/Signos

447. Dial.   Marque.   *MAHR-keh.*

448. For reception.   Para hablar con la recepción.
PAH-rah ah-BLAHR kohn lah reh-sehp-see-OHN.

449. For an outside line.   Para una línea exterior.
PAH-rah OO-nah LEE-neh-ah ehks-teh-ree-OHR.

450. Do not disturb.   No molestar.   *noh moh-lehs-TAHR.*

451. No food in the room.
Prohibido comer en la habitación.   *proh-ee-BEE-doh koh-MEHR en lah ah-bee-tah see-OHN.*

452. Fire door.   Puerta de incendios.
PWEHR-tah deh een-SEHN-dee-ohs.

453. Emergency exit.   Salida de emergencia.
sah-LEE-dah deh eh-mehr-hehn-SEE-ah.

Vacancy (rooms, bed).   Habitaciones, camas.
ah-bee-tah-cee-OHN-ehs, KAHM-ahs.

No vacancy.   Completo.   *kohm-PLEH-toh.*

Remember that outside the United States, the first floor is not the ground floor, but the first floor up.

Many of the hotels will have cards with information on them in Spanish and several other languages. Many also use icons to help communicate better.

Checking Out/Irse

454. When do I (we) have to check out?
¿A qué hora hay que dejar la habitación?   *ah keh OH-rah i keh deh-HAHR lah ah-bee-tah-see-OHN?*

455. I am (We) are leaving now.
Me voy (Nos vamos) ahora.
meh boy (nohs BAH-mohs) ah-OH-rah.

456. I would like to pay the bill.
Quiero pagar la cuenta.
kee-EH-roh pah-GAHR lah KWEHN-tah.

457. Can I leave my backpack at the reception desk until tonight?
¿Puedo dejar mi mochila en la recepción hasta esta noche?
PWEH-doh deh-HAHR mee moh-CHEE-lah ehn lah reh-sehp-see-OHN AHS-tah EHS-tah NOH-cheh?

458. Can you call a taxi for me, please?
¿Puede llamar a un taxi, por favor?   *PWEH-deh yah-mahr ah OON TAK-see pohr fah-BOHR.*

Apartment/*El Apartamento*

459. I want a furnished apartment.
   Quiero un apartamento amueblado.   *kee-EH-roh*
   oon ah-pahr-tah-MEHN-toh ah-mweh-BLAH-doh.

460. I want a living room, _____ bedrooms.
   Quiero una sala, _____ alcobas.
   kee-EH-roh OO-nah SAH-lah, _____ahl-KOH-bahs.

461. A dining room, a kitchen.
   Un comedor, una cocina.
   oon koh-meh-DOHR, OO-nah koh-SEE-nah.

462. A patio, a private bath.
   Un patio, un baño particular.
   oon PAH-tee-oh, oon BAH-nyoh pahr-tee-koo-LAHR.

463. Is the linen included?
   ¿Eso incluye sábanas y mantelería?   *EH-soh een-*
   CLOO-yeh SAH-bah-nahs ee mahn-teh-leh-REE-ah.?

464. How much is it per month?   ¿Cuánto es por mes?
   KWAHN-toh ehs pohr mehs?

Quick & to the Point

bedroom.	el dormitorio.	*ehl dohr-mee-tohr-EE-oh.*
kitchen.	la cocina.	*lah koh-SEE-nah.*
bathroom.	el cuarto de baño.	*ehl KWAHR-toh deh BAH-nyoh.*
parking.	el aparcamiento.	*ehl ah-pahr-kah-mee-EHN-toh.*

465. Where do we pick up the keys?

¿Dónde recogemos las llaves?

DOHN-deh reh-coh-HEH-mohs lahs YAH-behs?

466. What day does the cleaner come?

¿Qué día viene la señora de limpieza?   *keh DEE-ah bee-EH-neh lah seh-nyor-ah de leem-pee-EH-sah?*

467. When do I put out the trash?

¿Cuándo hay que sacar la basura?

KWAHN-doh i keh SAH-kahr lah bah-SOO-rah?

468. The blankets, silverware, and dishes.

Las mantas (las cobijas), los cubiertos, la vajilla.

lahs MAHN-tahs (las ko-BEE-hahs), lohs koo-bee-EHR-tohs, lah bah-HEE-yah.

469. Washing machine, refrigerator, freezer.

La lavadora, el refrigerador, el congelador.

lah lah-bah-DOH-rah, ehl reh-free-heh-rah-DOHR, ehl con-heh-lah-DOHR.

470. Can I get a maid?

¿Puedo conseguir una empleada doméstica?

PWEH-doh kohn-seh-GEER OO-nah ehm-pleh-AH-da doh-MEHS-tee-kah?

471. Do you know a good cook?

¿Conoce usted a una buena cocinera?

koh-NOH-seh oos-TEHD ah OO-nah boo-EH-nah koh-see-NEH-rah?

472. Where can I contact you?

¿Dónde me puedo poner en contacto con usted?

DOHN-deh meh PWEH-doh poh-NEHR ehn kon-TAHK-toh kon oos-TEHD?

473. How does the stove (oven, water heater, microwave) work?

¿Cómo funciona la estufa, (el horno, el calentador, el microondas)?   *KOH-moh foon-see-OH-nah lah ehs-TOO-fah,(ehl OHR-noh, ehl kah-lehn-tah-DOHR, ehl mee-croh-OHN-dahs)?*

474. The _____ has broken down.

_____se ha estropeado.

_____*seh ah ehs-troh-peh-AH-doh.*

475. Where can I rent a garage?

¿Dónde puedo alquilar un garaje?   *DOHN-deh PWEH-doh ahl-kee-LAHR oon gah-RAH-heh?*

Titles in Spanish

Mr.	Sr. (señor).	*seh-NYOR.*
Mrs.	Sra. (señora).	*seh-NYOR-ah.*
Miss	Srta. (señorita).	*seh-nyor-EE-tah.*

You may also hear these additional titles used before a first name. It is a title of respect used for people whom you refer to by their first name. We don't really have an equivalent in America, but it is somewhat like Miss Jane or Mr. John.

don	*dohn*
doña	*DOH-nya*

---

476. We will return at 12:30 p.m.

Volvemos a las doce y media de la tarde.

bohl-BEH-mohs ah lahs DOH-seh ee MEH-dee-ah deh lah TAHR-deh.

Restaurant/*El Restaurante*

477. Where is there a good restaurant?

¿Dónde hay un buen restaurante?

DOHN-deh i oon bwehn rehs-tahw-RAHN-te?

478. Is there a traditional local style restaurant near here?

¿Hay cerca de aquí un restaurante típico? *i SEHR-ka deh ah-kee oon rehs-tahw-RAHN-te TEE-pee-coh?*

479. Chinese restaurant. Un restaurante chino.

oon rehs-tahw-RAHN-te CHEE-noh.

480. Greek restaurant. Un restaurante griego.

oon rehs-tahw-RAHN-te gree-EH-goh.

Quick & to the Point

restaurant. el restaurante. *ehl rehs-tahw-RAHN-teh.*

nearby. cercano. *sehr-KAH-noh.*

lunch. el almuerzo. *ehl ahl-MWEHR-soh.*

breakfast. el desayuno. *ehl deh-sah-YOO-noh.*

dinner. la cena. *lah SEH-nah.*

inexpensive. barato. *bah-RAH-toh.*

elegant. elegante. *ehl-eh-GAHN-teh.*

Getting what you want.

You can use the following structures (sprinkled with *por favor* and *gracias*—please and thank you) for a number of situations:

I want ... Me gusta ... *meh GOOS-tah ...*
+ any noun or verb.

or I don't want ... No me gusta...
noh meh GOOS-tah ...

I would like ... Me gustaría ...
meh goos-tah-REE-ah ... + any noun or verb.

or I wouldn't like ... No me gustaría ...
noh meh goos-tah-REE-ah ...

EXAMPLE: Me gusta comer. I like to eat.
Me gusta el helado. I like ice cream.
Me gustaría comer. I would like to eat.
Me gustaría un helado. I would like ice cream.

---

481. Italian restaurant. Un restaurante italiano.
oon rehs-tahw-RAHN-te ee-tah-lee-AH-noh.

482. Vegetarian. Un restaurante vegetariano.
oon rehs-tahw-RAHN-te veh-heh-tah-ree-AH-noh.

483. Inexpensive. Un restaurante barato.
oon rehs-tahw-RAHN-te bah-RAH-toh.

484. A hamburger stand. Una hamburguesería.
OO-nah ahm-boor-geh-seh-REE-ah.

485. Fast food restaurant.
Un restaurante de comida rápida. *oon rehs-tahw-RAHN-te deh koh-MEE-dah RAH-pee-dah.*

486. An ice cream shop. Una heladería.
OO-nah eh-lah-deh-REE-ah.

487. Pizzeria. Una pizzería. *OO-nah pee-seh-REE-ah.*

488. Steakhouse. Una churrasquería.
OO-nah choo-rrahs-keh-REE-ah.

489. For breakfast, lunch, dinner.
Para el desayuno, el almuerzo, la cena.
PAH-rah ehl deh-sah-YOO-noh, ehl ahl-MWEHR-soh, lah SEH-nah.

490. A sandwich. Un sándwich. *oon SAHN-weech.*

Getting Seated and Ordering/Sentarse y Ordenar

491. Between what hours is dinner served?
¿Entre qué horas se sirve la cena?
EHN-treh keh OH-ras seh SEER-veh lah SEH-nah?

492. Can we have lunch now?
¿Podemos almorzar ahora?
poo-DEH-mohs ahl-mohr-SAHR ah-HOH-rah?

493. There are two of us. Somos dos.
SOH-mohs dohs.

Quick & to the Point

I would like a table for two.　Me gustaría una mesa para dos.
meh goos-tah-REE-ah OO-nah MEHS-ah PAH-rah dohs.

Are there any free tables?　¿Hay mesas libres?
I MEHS-ahs LEE-brehs?

The menu, please.　El menú (la carta), por favor.
ehl meh-NOO (lah KAHR-tah), pohr fah-BOHR.

The bill, please.　La cuenta, por favor.
lah KWEHN-tah, pohr fah-BOHR.

Can I pay by credit card?　¿Puedo pagar con tarjeta de crédito?
PWEH-doh PAH-gahr kohn tahr-HEH-tah deh KREH-dee-toh?

494. The head waiter, waiter, waitress.

El jefe de camareros (meseros), el camarero
(mesero), la camarera (mesera).　*ehl HEH-feh deh
ka-mah REH-rohs (meh-SEH-rohs), ehl kah-mah-REH-roh
(meh-SEH-roh),lah kah-mah-REH-rah (meh-SEH-rah).*

495. For breakfast, lunch, dinner.

Para el desayuno, el almuerzo, la cena.
*PAH-rah ehl deh-sah-YOO-noh, ehl ahl-MWEHR-soh,
lah SEH-nah.*

496. Give me a table near the window.

Déme una mesa cerca de la ventana.　*DEH-meh
OO-nah MEH-sah SEHR-kah deh lah behn-TAH-nah.*

497. In a non-smoking section.

En una zona de no fumadores.
ehn OO-nah SOH-nah deh noh foo-mah-DOH-rehs.

69

RESTAURANT

498. I'm sorry. We are very busy (full).
Lo siento. Tenemos mucha gente (está lleno).
loh see-EHN-toh. Teh-NEH-mohs MOO-chah HEHN-teh (ehs-TAH YEH-noh).

499. We'll have a free table in _____ minutes.
Tendremos una mesa libre en _____ minutos.
tehn-DREH-mohs OO-nah MEH-sah LEE-breh ehn _____ mee-NOO-tohs.

500. Can we sit outside? ¿Podríamos sentarnos fuera?
poh-DREE-ah-mohs sehn-TAHR-nohs FWEH-rah?

501. Waiter! ¡Camarero! (¡Mesero!, ¡Mozo!)
kah-mah-REH-roh! (meh-SEH-roh! MOH-soh!)

502. Is this table reserved? ¿Está reservada esta mesa?
ehs-TAH reh-sehr-BAH-dah EHS-tah MEH-sah?

503. Bring me the menu. Tráigame la carta.
TRI-gah meh la KAHR-tah.

504. The wine list. La carta de vinos.
lah KAHR-tah deh BEE-nohs.

505. I'll have a bottle (glass, carafe) of _____.
Tomaré una botella (un vaso, una garrafa) de
_____. *toh-mah-REH OO-nah boh-TEH-yah (oon BAH-soh, OO-nah ga-RRAH-fah) deh.*

506. Do you have a set menu?
¿Tienen el menú del día?
tee-EH-nehn ehl meh-NOO dehl DEE-ah?

507. Could you tell me what _____ is?
¿Podría decirme lo que _____ es?
poh-DREE-ah deh-SEER-meh loh keh _____ ehs?

508. Can you recommend some typical local dishes?
¿Puede recomendarme algunos platos típicos de la zona?
PWEH-deh reh-coh-mehn-DAHR-meh ahl-GOO-nohs PLAH-tohs TEE-pee-cohs deh lah SOH-nah?

509. What are the specials today?
¿Cuáles son los platos especiales del día? *KWAH-lehs sohn lohs PLAH-tohs ehs-peh-see-AH-lehs dehl DEE-ah?*

510. What do you suggest for an appetizer?
¿Qué aperitivos me recomienda?
keh ah-peh-ree-TEE-bohs meh reh-coh-mee-EHN-dah?

511. As a starter (main course, side order).
De primero (de segundo, guarnición). *deh pree-MEH-roh (deh seh-GOON-doh, gwar-nee-see-OHN.)*

512. Are you ready to order? ¿Van a pedir ya?
bahn ah peh-DEER-yah?

513. What would you like? ¿Qué va a desear?
keh bah ah deh-seh-AHR?

514. What would you like to drink?
¿Qué quiere de beber?
keh kee-EH-reh deh beh-BEHR?

515. I recommend _____. Le recomiendo _____.
leh reh-koh-mee-EHN-doh_____.

516. We haven't got _____. No tenemos _____.
noh teh-NEH-mohs _____.

517. That will take _____ minutes.
Eso tardará _____ minutos.
EH-soh tahr-dah-RAH _____ mee-NOO-tohs.

518. Can I change this for (fruta)?
¿Se puede cambiar esto por (fruta)?   seh PWEH-deh kahm-bee-AHR EHS-toh pohr (FROO-tah)?

519. Enjoy your meal.   *Que le aproveche.*
keh leh ah-proh-BEH-cheh.

520. Not too spicy.   *No muy picante.*
noh mwee pee-KAHN-teh.

521. A napkin, a glass.   *Una servilleta, un vaso.*
OO-nah sehr-vee-YEH-tah, oon BAH-soh.

Cheers, Etc.

Eating is a social experience in Spanish-speaking countries. Meals are generally more leisurely and a lot of conversation goes on. Be sure to use some of these expressions to your fellow diners.

Enjoy your meal. Buen provecho.

Que le aproveche.

Cheers! ¡Salud!

¡Chin! ¡Chin!

¡Toda la suerte!

¡A su (tú) salud!

---

522. A plate, a knife.   Un plato, un cuchillo.
oon PLAH-toh, oon koo-CHEE-yoh.

523. A fork, a large spoon.   Un tenedor, una cuchara.
oon teh-neh-DOHR, OO-nah koo-CHAH-rah.

524. A teaspoon.   Una cucharita.
OO-nah koo-cha-REE-tah.

525. The bread, the butter.   El pan, la mantequilla.
ehl pahn, lah mahn-teh-KEE-yah.

526. The cream, the sugar.   La crema, el azúcar.
lah KREH-mah, ehl ah-SOO-kahr.

527. The salt, pepper.   La sal, la pimienta.
lah sahl, lah pee-mee-EHN-tah.

528. The sauce, the vinegar, the (olive) oil.
La salsa, el vinagre, el aceite (de oliva).
lah SAHL-sah, ehl bee-NAH-greh, ehl ah-SEH-ee-teh.
(deh oh-LEE-vah).

529. An ashtray, toothpick.   Un cenicero, un palillo.
oon seh-nee-SEH-roh, oon pah-LEE-yoh.

530. I have had enough, thanks.   Basta, gracias.
BAHS-tah, GRAH-see-ahs.

531. This is not clean.   Esto no está limpio.
ehs-TOH noh ehs-TAH LEEM-pee-oh.

532. It is dirty.   Está sucio.   *ehs-TAH soo-PEE-oh.*

533. Waiter (waitress), there's something in my soup.
Camarero/a, hay algo en mi sopa.
Kah-mah-REH-roh/ah, i AHL-goh ehn mee SOH-pah.

73

534. A little more of this. Un poco más de esto.
oon POH-coh mahs deh EHS-toh.

535. I like it rare (medium, well done).
La prefiero bien cruda (poco cruda or regular, bien cocida).
lah preh-fee-EH-roh bee-EHN KROO-dah (POH-coh KROO-dah, or reh-GOO-lahr, bee-EHN koh-SEE-dah).

536. This is overdone (underdone).
Esto está demasiado hecho (crudo).   *EHS-toh ehs-TAH deh-mah-see-AH-doh EH-choh (KROO-doh).*

537. That is not cooked enough.
Eso no está bastante cocido.
EH-soh noh ehs-TAH-bahs-TAHN-teh koh-SEE-doh.

538. This is too tough (sweet, sour, bitter).
Esto está muy duro (dulce, amargo, ácido).
EHS-toh ehs-TAH- mwee DOO-roh (DOOL-seh, ah-MAHR-goh, AH-see-doh).

539. This is cold.   Esto está frío.
EHS-toh ehs-TAH FREE-oh.

540. This isn't fresh.   Esto no está fresco.
EHS-toh noh ehs-TAH FREHS-koh.

541. The food is cold.   La comida está fría.
lah koh-MEE-dah ehs-TAH FREE-ah.

542. Take it away.   Lléveselo.   *YEH-beh-seh-loh.*

543. Have you forgotten our drinks?
¿Se le han olvidado las bebidas?
seh leh ahn ohl-bee-DAH-doh lahs beh-BEE-dahs?

544. This is not what I ordered.   Esto no es lo que pedí.
EHS-toh noh ehs loh keh peh-DEE.

545. Do you have meals for diabetics?
¿Tienen comida para diabéticos?   *tee-EH-nehn koh-MEE-dah PAH-rah dee-ah-BEH-tee-kohs?*

546. I can't eat food containing _____.
No debo comer comida que tenga _____.
noh DEH-boh koh-MEHR koh-MEE-dah keh TEHN-gah _____.

547. I'm allergic to shellfish.
Soy alérgico a los mariscos.
Soy ah-LEHR-hee-koh ah lohss mah-REES-kohss.

548. Do you have children's portions?
¿Hacen porciones para niños?
AH-sehn pohr-see-OH-nehs PAH-rah NEE-nyohs?

549. Could we have a child's seat?
¿Podrían ponernos una sillita para niños?
poh DREE-ahn poh-NEHR-nohs OO-nah see-YEE-tah PAH-rah NEE-nyohs?

550. Where can I feed (change) the baby?
¿Dónde puedo darle de comer (cambiar) al niño/a?
DOHN-deh PWEH-doh DAHR-leh deh ko-MEHR (kahm-bee-AHR) ahl NEE-nyoh/nyah?

551. Where are the bathrooms?
¿Dónde están los servicios?
DOHN-deh ehs-TAHN lohs sehr-bee-SEE-ohs?

RESTAURANT

Leaving the Restaurant/*Saliendo del Restaurante*

552. The check, please.   La cuenta, por favor.
lah KWEHN-tah, pohr fah-BOHR.

553. Kindly pay at the cashier.
Haga el favor de pagar en la caja.   *AH-gah ehl
fah-BOHR deh pah-GAHR ehn-lah KAH-hah.*

554. Is the tip included?   ¿Está incluida la propina?
ehs-TAH-een-kloo-EE-dah lah proh-PEE-nah?

555. Keep the change.   El cambio es para usted.
ehl KAM-bee-oh ehs PAH-rah oos-TEHD.

556. There is a mistake in the bill.
Hay un error en la cuenta.
i oon eh-RROHR ehn lah KWEHN-tah.

557. What are these charges for?
¿Qué son estos cargos extras?
keh sohn EHS-tohs CAHR-gohs EHKS-trahs?

Delicious!   ¡Delicioso!   *deh-lee-see-OH-soh!*

Very tasty!   ¡Qué rico!   *keh REE-koh!*

Yummy!   ¡Qué sabroso!   *keh sah-BROH-soh!*

I love this food!   ¡Me encanta esta comida!
meh ehn-KAHN-tah EHS-tah koh-MEE-dah!

My compliments to the chef!
¡Felicitaciones al cocinero!
feh-lee-see-tah-see-OHN-ehs ahl coh-see-NEHR-oh!

Ordering Wine/Ordenando Vino

Generally expensive, but usually good choices:

house wine	vino de la casa
table wine	vino de mesa
local wine	vino local
regional wine	vino de la región

Wine types

red	vino tinto	**dry**	seco
white	vino blanco	**semi-dry**	semi-seco
rosé	vino rosado	**new wine**	vino joven
sparkling	espumoso	**full-bodied**	maduro
sweet	dulce		

Labels on Wine/Marcas de Vino

Gran Reserva: *wine that has been aged in storage for two years and three years in the bottle.*

Reserva: *wine that has been aged at least three years for red and two years for white.*

DOC: *highest quality guarantee for wine-making.*

DO: *high-quality standards for wine*

DOP: *next best quality, after DO*

CAFÉ

558. Is there a service charge?
¿Hay que pagar por el servicio?
I keh pah-GAHR pohr ehl serh-bee-SEE-oh?

559. Could I have a VAT receipt?
¿Podría darme un recibo con el IVA, por favor?
poh-DREE-ah DAHR-meh oon reh-SEE-boh kohn ehl ee-beh-ah, pohr fah-BOHR?

560. Can I pay with a credit card?
¿Puedo pagar con esta tarjeta de crédito?
PWEH-doh pah-GAHR kohn EHS-tah tahr-HEH-tah deh KREH-dee-toh?

561. That was a very good meal.
La comida estuvo muy buena.
lah koh-MEE-dah ehs-TOO-boh mwee BWEH-nah.

Café/El Café

562. Bartender. El barman. *ehl BAHR-mahn.*

563. Waiter, waitress. Mozo, moza.
MOH-soh, MOH-sah.

564. A cocktail. Un cóctel. *oon KOHK-tehl.*

565. A fruit drink. Una bebida de frutas.
OO-nah beh-BEE-dah deh FROO-tahs.

566. Ice water. Agua helada. *AH-gwah ee-LAH dah.*

567. A liqueur. Un licor. *oon lee-KOHR.*

568. Brandy. El aguardiente. *ehl ah-gwahr-dee-EHN-teh.*

78

> ## Quick & to the Point
>
> **Small draft beer.** Una caña. *OON-ah KA-nyah.*
>
> **A glass of tap water.** Un vaso de agua del grifo.
> *oon BAH-soh deh AH-gwah dehl GREE-foh.*
>
> **Is the water safe to drink?** ¿Es el agua potable?
> *ehs ehl AH-gwah poh-TAHB-leh?*
>
> **Cheers!** ¡Salud! *sah-LOOD!*

569. **Light (dark) beer.** Cerveza clara (oscura).
     sehr-BEE-sah KLAH-rah (ohs-KOO-rah).

570. **White (red) wine.** Vino blanco (tinto).
     BEE-noh BLAHN-koh (TEEN-toh).

571. **A soft drink.** Un refresco. *oon reh-FREHS-koh.*

572. **A bottle of _____.** Una botella de _____?
     OO-nah boh-TEH-yah deh _____.

573. **A glass of _____.** Un vaso de _____.
     oon BAH-soh deh _____.

574. **Let's have another.** Tomemos otro más.
     toh-MEH-mohs OH-troh mahs.

575. **Same again, please.** Otra de lo mismo.
     OH-trah deh loh MEES-moh.

Ordering Coffee

To get your coffee the way you enjoy it while in Spain, use these terms.

Coffee ... Café ... *kah-FEH* ...

black. solo. *SOH-loh.*

with a little milk. cortado. *kohr-TAH-doh.*

with a lot of milk. con leche. *kohn LEH-cheh.*

with sugar. con azúcar. *kohn ah-SOO-cahr.*

iced. con hielo. *kohn YEH-loh.*

American style. americano. *ah-mehr-ee-KAHN-oh.*

espresso. espreso. *ehs-PREH-soh.*

with a touch of brandy. carajillo. *kah-rah-HEE-yoh.*

instant coffee. Nescafé. *nehs-kah-FEH.*

decaffeinated. descafeinado. *dehs-kah-feh-NAH-doh.*

Food/Los Alimentos

A more extensive list of foods can be found on page 161.

This section has been alphabetized in Spanish to facilitate the tourist's reading of Spanish menus.

576. Olives. Aceitunas. *ah-seyh-TOO-nahs.*

577. Tuna. Atún. *ah-TOON.*

578. Roll. Bollo. *BOH-yoh.*

579. Pudding. Búdin. *BOO-deen.*

580. Donut (fried pastry). Buñuelo. *buh-nyoo-EH-loh.*

581. Peanuts. Cacahuates. *kah-cah-WAH-tehs.*

582. Coffee (with milk, cream). Café (con leche, crema). *kah-FEH (kohn LEH-cheh, KREH-mah).*

583. Black coffee. Café solo. *kah-FEH SOH-loh.*

584. Pumpkin or squash. Calabaza. *kah-lah-BAH-sah.*

585. (Chicken) broth. Caldo (de pollo). *KAL-doh (deh POH-yoh)*

586. Shrimp. Camarones. *kah-mah-ROH-nehs.*

587. Sweet potato. Camote, batata. *kah-MOH-teh, bah-TAH-tah.*

588. Crab. Cangrejo. *kahn-GREH-hoh.*

589. Meat. Carne. *KAHR-neh.*

590. (Roast, broiled) beef. Carne de vaca (asada, a la parrilla). *KAR-neh deh BAH-kah (ah-SAH-dah, ah lah pah-RREE-yah).*

591. Mutton. Carnero. *kahr-NEH-roh.*

592. Onion. Cebolla. *seh-BOH-yah.*

593. Cherry. Cereza. *seh-REH-sah.*

594. Mushroom. Champiñón. *cham-pee-NYOHN.*

595. Sausage. Chorizo. *choh-REE-soh.*

596. Chop. Chuleta. *choo-LEH-tah.*

597. Stew. Cocido. *koh-SEE-doh.*

598. Cabbage. Col. *kohl.*

599. Cauliflower. Coliflor. *koh-lee-FLOHR.*

600. Stewed fruit. Compota. *kohm-POH-tah.*

601. Rabbit. Conejo. *koh-NEH-hoh.*

602. Jam. Conserva. *kohn-SEHR-bah.*

603. Peach. Durazno. *doo-RAHS-noh.*

604. Meat pie. Empanada. *ehm-pah-NAH-dah.*

605. Pickles. Encurtidos, pepinillos.
ehn coor-TEE-dohs, peh-pee-NEE-yohs.

606. Salad. Ensalada. *ehn sah-LAH-dah.*

607. Hors d'oeuvres. Entremeses. *ehn-treh-MEH-sehs.*

608. Pickled fish. Escabeche. *ehs-kah-BEH-cheh.*

609. Asparagus. Espárragos. *ehs-PAH-rrah-gohs.*

610. Spinach. Espinacas. *ehs-pee-NAH-kahs.*

611. Meat stew. Estofado. *ehs-toh-FAH-doh.*

612. Pheasant. Faisán. *fi-SAHN.*

613. Cold cuts. Fiambres. *fee-AHM-brehs.*

614. Noodles. Fideos. *fee-DEH-ohs.*

615. **Tenderloin.** Filete. *fee-LEH-teh.*

616. **Custard.** Flan. *flahn.*

617. **Raspberry.** Frambuesa. *frahm-BWEH-sah.*

618. **Strawberry.** Fresa. *FREH-sah.*

619. **Beans.** Frijoles. *free-HOH-lehs*

620. **Chick peas.** Garbanzos. *gahr-BAHN-sohs.*

621. **Turkey.** Guajolote, pavo.
gwah-hoh-LOH-teh, pah-boh.

622. **Stew.** Guisado. *gee-SAH-doh.*

623. **Peas.** Guisantes. *gee-SAHN-tehs.*

624. **Guava.** Guayaba. *gwah-YAH-bah.*

625. **Green beans.** Habichuelas. *ah-bee-CHWEH-lahs.*

626. **Ice cream.** Helado. *eh-LAH-doh.*

627. **Ice cubes.** Hielo. *YEH-loh.*

628. **Liver.** Hígado. *EE-gah-doh.*

629. **Fig.** Higo. *EE-goh.*

630. **Mushrooms.** Hongos, setas. *OHN-gohs, she-tahs.*

631. **Eggs (fried with chile sauce).** Huevos a la
ranchera. *WEH-bohs ah lah rahn-CHEH-rah.*

632. **Hard-boiled eggs.** Huevos duros.
WEH-bohs DOO-rohs.

633. **Fried eggs.** Huevos fritos. *WEH-bohs FREE-tohs.*

634. **Scrambled eggs.** Huevos revueltos.
WEH-bohs reh-BWEL-tohs.

635. **Jelly.** Jalea. *hah-LEH-ah.*

83

636. Ham. Jamón. *hah-MOHN.*

637. Sherry. Jerez. *heh-REHS.*

638. Hash. Jigote. *hee-GOH-teh.*

639. Lobster. Langosta. *lahn-GOHS-tah.*

640. Milk (condensed, malted).
Leche (condensada, malteada).
LEH-cheh (kohn-dehn-SAH-dah, mahl-teh-AH-dah).

641. Lettuce. Lechuga. *leh-CHOO-gah.*

642. Vegetables. Legumbres. *leh-GOOM-brehs.*

643. Flounder. Lenguado. *lehn-GWAH-doh.*

644. Lentils. Lentejas. *lehn-TEH-hahs.*

645. Hare. Liebre. *lee-EH-breh.*

646. Lemon. Limón. *lee-MOHN.*

647. Lemonade. Limonada. *lee-moh-NAH-dah.*

648. Corn. Maíz. *mah-EES.*

649. Apple. Manzana. *mahn-SAH-nah.*

650. Almond paste. Mazapán. *mah-sah-PAHN*

651. Peach. Melocotón. *mehl-oh-coh-TOHN.*

652. Melon. Melón. *meh-LOHN.*

653. Vegetable soup. Menestra. *meh-NEHS-trah.*

654. Marmalade. Mermelada. *mehr-meh-LAH-dah.*

655. Bologna. Mortadela. *mohr-tah-DEH-lah.*

656. Mustard. Mostaza. *mohs-TAH-sah.*

657. Turnip.   Nabo.   *NAH-boh.*

658. Orange.   Naranja.   *nah-RAHN-hah.*

659. Orangeade.   Naranjada.   *nah-rahn-HAH-dah.*

660. Spanish custard.   Natilla.   *nah-TEE-yah.*

661. Nuts.   Nueces.   *noo-EH-sehs.*

662. Yam.   Ñame.   *NYAH-meh.*

663. Oysters.   Ostras.   *OHS-trahs.*

664. Rolls.   Panecillos.   *pah-neh-SEE-yohs.*

665. Potatoes.   Papas or patatas.   *PAH-pahs or pah-TAH-tahs.*

666. Raisins.   Pasas.   *PAH-sahs.*

667. Pastry.   Pasteles.   *pahs-TEH-lehs.*

668. Baked potato.   Patata al horno.   *pah-TAH-tah ahl OHR-noh.*

669. Turkey.   Pavo.   *PAH-boh.*

670. Cucumbers.   Pepinos.   *peh-PEE-nohs.*

671. Pear.   Pera.   *PEH-rah.*

672. Perch.   Perca.   *PEHR-kah.*

673. Partridge.   Perdiz.   *pehr-DEES.*

674. Parsley.   Perejil.   *peh-reh-HEEL.*

675. Fried fish.   Pescado frito.   *pehs-KAH-doh FREE-toh.*

676. Hash.   Picadillo.   *pee-kah-DEE-yoh.*

677. Peppers.   Pimientos.   *pee-mee-EHN-tohs.*

678. Pineapple. Piña. *pee-nya.*

679. Bananas. Plátanos. *PLAH-tah-nohs.*

680. Chicken. Pollo. *POH-yoh.*

681. Broiled (grilled) chicken. Pollo a la parilla.
POH-yoh ah lah pah-REE-ya.

682. Dessert. Postre. *POHS-treh.*

683. Stew. Puchero. *poo-CHEH-roh.*

684. Pork. Puerco, cerdo. *PWEHR-coh, CEHR-doh.*

685. Pudding. Pudín. *poo-DEEN.*

686. Mashed potatoes. Puré de papas.
poo-REH deh-PAH-pahs.

687. Cheese. Queso. *KEH-soh.*

688. Radishes. Rábanos. *RAH-bah-nohs.*

689. Slice. Rebanada. *reh bah-NAH-dah.*

690. Cottage cheese. Requesón. *reh-keh-SOHN.*

691. Kidneys. Riñones. *Ree-NYOH-nehs.*

692. Haddock. Róbalo. *ROH-bah-loh.*

693. Roast beef. Rosbif. *rohs-BEEF.*

694. Sausage. Salchicha. *sahl-CHEE-chah.*

695. Salami. Salchichón. *sahl-chee-CHOHN.*

696. Salmon. Salmón. *sahl-MOHN.*

697. Chopped meat. Salpicón. *sahl-pee-KOHN.*

698. Sauce. Salsa. *SAHL-sah.*

699. Watermelon. Sandía. *sahn-DEE-ah.*

700. Sardine. Sardina. *sahr-DEE-nah.*

701. Brains. Sesos. *SEH-sohs.*

702. Mushrooms. Setas. *SEH-tahs.*

703. Clear soup. Sopa clara. *SOH-pah KLAH-rah.*

704. Thick soup. Sopa espesa. *SOH-pah ehs-PEH-sah.*

705. Sherbet. Sorbete. *sohr-BEH-teh.*

706. Pie or tart. Tarta. *TAHR-tah.*

707. Tea. Té. *teh.*

708. Veal (Cutlet). (Chuleta de) ternera. *(choo-LEH-tah deh) tehr-NEH-rah.*

709. Bacon. Tocino. *toh-SEE-noh.*

710. Tomato. Tomate. *toh-MAH-teh.*

711. Grapefruit. Toronja. *toh-ROHN-hah.*

712. Cake. Torta. *TOHR-tah.*

713. Omelet. Tortilla. *tohr-TEE-yah.*

714. Toast. Tostada. *tohs-TAH-dah.*

715. Trout. Trucha. *TROO-chah.*

716. Nougat. Turrón. *too-RROHN*

717. Grapes. Uvas. *OO-bahs.*

718. Venison. Venado. *beh-NAH-doh.*

719. Green leafy vegetables. Verduras. *behr-DOO-rahs.*

720. Carrots. Zanahorias. *sah-nah-oh-REE-ahs.*

Church/*La Iglesia*

721. Is there a synagogue? ¿Hay una sinagoga?
I OO-nah see-nah-GOH-gah?

722. Where is the nearest Catholic church?
¿Dónde está la iglesia católica más cercana?
DOHN-deh ehs-TAH lah ee-GLEH-see-ah cah-TOH-lee-ka mahs sehr-KAH-nah?

723. We wish to attend a Protestant service. Queremos
asistir a un servicio protestante. *keh-REH-mohs ah-sees-TEER ah oon sehr-bee-SEE-oh proh-tehs-TAHN-teh.*

724. Where is there a service in English?
¿Dónde predican en inglés?
DOHN-deh preh-DEE-kahn ehn een-GLEHS?

725. For Baptists, for Methodists.
Para bautistas, para metodistas.
PAH-rah baw-TEES-tahs, PAH-rah meh-toh-DEES-tahs.

726. For Presbyterians. Para presbiterianos.
PAH-rah prehs-bee-teh-ree-AH-nohs.

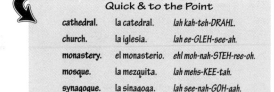

Quick & to the Point

cathedral.	la catedral.	*lah kah-teh-DRAHL.*
church.	la iglesia.	*lah ee-GLEH-see-ah.*
monastery.	el monasterio.	*ehl moh-nah-STEH-ree-oh.*
mosque.	la mezquita.	*lah mehs-KEE-tah.*
synagogue.	la sinagoga.	*lah see-nah-GOH-gah.*
chapel.	la capilla.	*lah kah-PEE-yah.*

727. I want a priest (minister).

Quiero hablar con un cura (un ministro).   *kee-EH-roh ah-BLAHR kohn oon KOO-rah (oon mee-NEES-troh).*

728. When is the service (Mass)?

¿A qué hora es el servicio (la misa)?   *ah keh OH-rah ehs ehl sehr-BEE-see-oh (lah MEE-sah)?*

729. Is there an English-speaking priest?

¿Hay algún cura que hable inglés?
i ahl-GOON KOO-rah keh AH-bleh een-GLEHS?

Some words you may hear when visiting churches:

God	Díos	*DEE-ohs*
altar	el altar	*ehl ahl-TAHR*
bells	las campanas	*lahs kahm-PAHN-ahs*
cloister	el claustro	*ehl KLOW-stroh*
cross	la cruz	*lah kroos*
crypt	la cripta	*lah KREEP-tah*
dome	la cúpula	*lah KOO-poo-lah*
organ	el órgano	*ehl OHR-gah-noh*
pulpit	el púlpito	*ehl POOL-pee-toh*
relic	la reliquia	*lah reh-LEE-kee-ah*
treasury	el tesoro	*ehl teh-SOH-roh*
saint	el/la santo/a	*ehl/lah SAHN-toh/tah*

Entertainment and Recreation/*El entretenimiento y los pasatiempos*

Sightseeing/Visitas a Puntos de Interés

730. I want a guide who speaks English.

Deseo un guía que hable inglés.   *deh-SEH-oh oon GEE-ah keh ah-bleh een-GLEHS.*

731. What do you charge an hour?

¿Cuánto cobra usted por hora?   *KWAHN-toh KOH-brah oos-TEHD pohr OH-rah?*

Quick & to the Point

Where is _____?   ¿Dónde está _____?
DOHN-deh ehs-TAH?

What days is it open?   ¿Qué días está abierto?
keh DEE-ahs ehs-TAH ah-bee-EHR-toh?

What time does it open?   ¿A qué hora abre?
a keh OH-rah AH-breh?

What time does it close?   ¿A qué hora cierra?
a keh OH-rah see-EH-rah?

How much is the admission?   ¿Cuánto es la entrada?
KWAHN-toh ehs lah ehn-TRAH-dah?

Do you have guided tours?   ¿Tiene una visita con guía?
tee-EH-neh OO-nah bee-SEE-tah kohn GEE-ah?

Are there guides in English?   ¿Hay guías en inglés?
i GEE-ahs ehn een-GLEHS?

732. I am interested in archeology (art).

Me interesa la arqueología (el arte).   *meh een-teh-REH-sah lah ahr-keh-oh-loh-HEE-ah (ehl AHR-teh).*

733. Native arts and crafts.   Las artes y obras indígenas.   *lahs AHR-tehs ee OH-brahs een-DEE-heh-nahs.*

734. Painting, ruins.   La pintura, las ruinas.
lah peen-TOO-rah, lahs roo-EE-nahs.

735. Sculpture.   La escultura.   *lah ehs-cool-TOO-rah.*

736. I'll have time to visit the museums.

Tendré tiempo de visitar los museos.   *tehn-DREH tee-EHM-poh deh bee-see-TAHR lohs moo-SEH-ohs.*

737. The cathedral.   La catedral.   *lah kah-teh-DRAHL.*

738. The bull ring.   La plaza de toros.
lah PLAH-sah deh TOH-rohs.

739. The library, the monastery.
La biblioteca, el monasterio.
lah bee-blee-oh-TEH-kah, ehl moh-nahs-TEH-ree-oh.

740. The park, the palace.   El parque, el palacio.
ehl PAHR-keh, ehl pah-LAH-see-oh.

741. Is it open (still)?   ¿Está abierta (todavía)?
ehs-TAH-ah-bee-EHR-tah (toh-dah-BEE-ah)?

742. How long does it stay open?
¿Hasta qué hora está abierto?
AHS-tah keh OH-rah ehs-TAH ah-bee-EHR-toh?

743. How long must we wait?
¿Cuánto tiempo tenemos que esperar?   *KWAHN-toh tee-EHM-poh teh-NEH-mohs keh ehs-peh-RAHR?*

744. Where is the entrance (exit)?
¿Dónde está la entrada (la salida)?   *DOHN-deh
ehs-TAH lah ehn-TRAH-dah (lah sah-LEE-dah)?*

745. What is the entrance fee?
¿Cuánto se paga por entrar?
KWAHN-toh seh PAH-gah pohr ehn-TRAHR?

746. Do we need a guide? ¿Necesitamos un guía?
neh-seh-see-TAH-mohs oon GEE-ah?

747. How much is the catalog (guide book)?
¿Cuánto cuesta el catálogo (la guía)?   *KWAHN-toh
KWEHS-tah ehl kah-TAH-loh-goh (lah GEE-ah)?*

748. May I take photographs?
¿Se permite sacar fotografías?
seh pehr-MEE-teh sah-KAHR foh-toh-grah-FEE-ahs?

749. Do you sell postcards (souvenirs)?
¿Vende postales (recuerdos)?
BEHN-deh pohs-TAH-lehs (reh-KWEHR-dohs)?

750. Do you have a book in English about _____?
¿Tiene un libro en inglés sobre _____?   *tee-EH-neh
oon LEE-broh ehn een-GLEHS SOH-breh _____?*

751. Take me back to the hotel now.   Lléveme al hotel
ahora.   *YEH-beh-meh ahl oh-TEHL ah-OH-rah.*

752. Go back by way of _____? ¿Regreso por _____?
reh-GREH-soh pohr _____?

Amusements/Las Diversiones

753. What is there to do today? ¿Qué diversiones hay
para hoy?   *keh dee-behr-see-OH-nehs i PAH-rah oy?*

Signs You Might See

Abierto. Open.
Aseos. Toilets.
Cerrado. Closed.
Entrada. Entrance.
Entrada gratis. Free admission.
No tocar. Don't touch.
No Flash. Don't use flash.
Prohibido Comer. No eating.
Prohibido el paso. No entry.
Prohibido fumar. No smoking.
Prohibido pisar la hierba. Keep off the grass.
Prohibido tomar fotos. No photography.
Salida. Exit.
Salida de Emergencia. Emergency Exit.
Servicios. Toilets.

754. **A bull fight, a concert.** Una corrida de toros, un concierto. *OO-nah koh-REE-dah deh TOH-rohs, oon kohn-see-EHR-toh.*

755. **Movies, native dances.** Las películas, los bailes populares. *lahs peh-LEE-koo-lahs, lohs BI-lehs poh-poo-LAH-rehs.*

756. **The beach, the pool.** La playa, la piscina. *lah PLAH-yah, lah pee-SEE-nah.*

Quick & to the Point

to play. jugar. *hoo-GAHR.*

checkers. las damas. *lahs DAH-mahs.*

cards. los naipes, las cartas.
lohs NI-pehs, lahs KAHR-tahs.

chess. el ajedrez. *ehl ah-heh-DREHS.*

basketball. el baloncesto. *ehl bah-lohn-SEHS-toh.*

soccer. el fútbol. *ehl FOOT-bohl.*

football. el fútbol americano.
ehl FOOT-bohl ah-meh-ree-KAH-noh.

video games. los videojuegos. *lohs bee-dee-oh-HWEH-gohs.*

757. Tennis (courts), golf (course). La cancha de tenis,
la cancha de golf. *lah KAHN-chah deh the-NEES,
lah KAHN-chah deh-gohlf.*

758. A club, the opera, the theatre. Una discoteca, la
ópera, el teatro. *OO-nah dees-koh-TEH-kah, lah
OH-peh-rah, ehl teh-AH-troh.*

759. Is there a matinée? ¿Hay función esta tarde?
I foon-see-OHN EHS-tah TAHR-deh?

760. When does the performance start?
¿A qué hora comienza la función?
ah keh OH-rah koh-mee-EHN-sah lah foon-see-OHN?

761. The show is at about 10. Se presenta el espectáculo a eso de las diez. *seh preh-SEHN-tah ehl
ehs-pehk-TAH-koo-loh ah EH-soh deh lahs dee-EHS.*

762. Cover charge, minimum.

El precio de admisión, el mínimo.   *ehl PREH-see-oh deh ahd-mee-see-OHN, elh MEE-nee-moh.*

763. Where can we go to dance?

¿A dónde podemos ir a bailar?   *ah DOHN-deh poh-DEH-mohs eer ah BI-lahr?*

764. What should I wear?

¿Qué clase de traje debo llevar?   *keh KLAH-seh deh TRAH-heh DEH-boh YEH-bahr?*

765. Do you have any seats for tonight?

¿Hay asientos para esta noche?   *i ah-see-EHN-tohs PAH-rah EHS-tah NOH-cheh?*

766. An orchestra seat, reserved seat.

Una butaca, un asiento reservado.   *OO-nah boo-TAH-ca, oon ah-see-EHN-toh reh-sehr-BAH-doh.*

767. In the balcony, a box.   En el anfiteatro, un palco.

ehn ehl ahn-fee-teh-AH-troh, oon PAHL-koh.

768. The checkroom, the usher.

El vestuario, el acomodador.   *ehl behs-too-AH-ree-oh, ehl ah-koh-moh-dah-DOHR.*

769. Can I see (hear) well from there?

¿Puedo ver (oír) bien desde allí?   *PWEH-doh behr (oh-EER) bee-EHN DEHS-deh ah-YEE?*

770. Not too near (far).   No muy cerca (lejos).

noh mwee SEHR-kah (LEH-hohs).

771. The music is excellent.   La música es excelente.

lah MOO-see-kah ehs ehk-seh-LEHN-teh.

In many Spanish-speaking countries including Spain, Mexico, Peru, Colombia, Venezuela, and Ecuador, you can attend a bullfight. While the sport is controversial, it still enjoys immense popularity in many places. If you decide to attend one, here are a few terms you will need.

Bandillero: a bullfighter's assistant who weakens the bull for the main bullfighter

Capote: a cape that is magenta and yellow used by "bandilleros" to attract the bulls to study for the fight; "matadors" then use the cape to attract the bull for the two to fight

Corrida: bullfight

Corrida de toros: the expert level of bullfighting

Espada: a sword, or another term for "matador" used in Spain

Matador: the bullfighter; in Spain and Mexico, bullfighters or "matadors" are considered national celebrities like American national sports heros

Muleta: a red cape over a stick that the "matador" uses at the end of the fight before he kills the bull with a sword

Picador: a mounted fighter on horseback with a spear, or "vara," who injures the bull to weaken it for the bullfigher to perform passes

Torero: a bullfighter

Vara: a spear used by a "picador"

772. This is very entertaining (funny).
Esto es muy divertido (cómico). *EHS-toh ehs mwee dee-behr-TEE-doh (KOH-mee-koh).*

773. May I have this dance? ¿Me permite esta pieza?
meh pehr-MEE-teh EHS-tah pee-EH-sah?

Movies and Television/*El Cine y La Television*

774. I feel like going to a comedy.
Tengo ganas de ir a una comedia. *TEHN-goh GAH-nahs deh eer ah OO-nah koh-MEH-dee-ah.*

775. Who is in it? ¿Quién actúa? *kee-EHN ahk-TOO-ah?*

776. Who is it directed by? ¿Quién la dirige?
kee-EHN lah dee-REE-heh?

777. I want to see an action film.
Quiero ver una película de acción. *kee-EH-roh behr OO-nah peh-LEE-koo-lah deh ahk-see-OHN.*

778. I don't like amateur film.
No me gusta el cine amateur.
noh meh GOOS-tah ehl SEE-neh ah-mah-teh-OOR.

779. Animated films, art films.
Las películas de dibujos animados, los filmes de autor.
lahs peh-LEE-koo-lahs deh dee-BOO-hohs ah-nee-MAH-dohs, lohs FEEL-mehs deh ah-oo-TOHR.

780. Documentary, drama. El documental, el drama.
ehl doh-koo-mehn-TAHL, ehl DRAH-mah.

Quick & to the Point

Turn on the television.   Encienda el televisor.
ehn-see-EHN-dah ehl teh-leh-bee-SOHR.

Turn off the television.   Apague el televisor.
ah-PAH-geh ehl tel-leh-bee-SOHR.

Change the channel.   Cambie el canal.
KAHM-bee-eh ehl kah-NAHL.

What's playing at the movies tonight?
¿Qué película dan en el cine esta noche?
keh peh-LEE-koo-lah dahn ehn ehl SEE-neh ESH-tah NOH-cheh?

Can I buy a ticket for the movie?
¿Puedo comprar una entrada para la película?   *PWEH-doh
kohm-PRAHR OO-nah ehn-TRAH-dah PAH-rah lah peh-LEE-koo-lah?*

781. Horror movie, period dramas.

El cine de terror, el cine de época.   *ehl SEE-neh deh
teh-RROHR, ehl SEE-neh deh EH-poh-kah.*

782. Realism, science fiction.

El cine realista, el cine de ciencia ficción.
*ehl SEE-neh reh-ah-LEES-tah, ehl SEE-neh deh see-
EHN-see-ah feek-see-OHN.*

783. Thrillers, war films.

El cine de suspenso, el cine bélico.   *ehl SEE-neh deh
soos-PEHN-soh, ehl SEE-neh BEH-lee-koh.*

784. Is it subtitled in English?

¿Tiene subtítulos en inglés?
tee-EH-neh soob-TEE-too-lohs ehn een-GLEHS?

A play or concert is performed in a **teatro** (teh-AH-troh).

A movie is shown at the **cine** (SEE-neh).

785. Is there an English channel? ¿Hay un canal inglés?
i oon kah-NAHL een-GLEHS?

786. Do you have a TV guide?
¿Tiene una guía de televisión?
tee-EH-neh OO-nah GEE-ah deh teh-leh bee-see-OHN?

787. The news, reporter. El noticiero, el (la) periodista.
ehl noh-tee-see-EH-roh, ehl (lah) peh-ree-oh-DEES-tah.

788. Commercial, game show.
El anuncio comercial, el concurso. *ehl ah-NOON-see-oh koh-mehr-see-AHL, ehl kon-KOOR-soh.*

789. The soap opera, the musical.
La telenovela, el musical.
lah teh-leh-noh-BEH-lah, ehl moo-see-KAHL.

790. The cast, the script. El elenco, el guión.
ehl eh-LEHN-koh, ehl gee-OHN.

791. Singer, actor, actress.
El (la) cantante, el actor, la actriz. *ehl (lah) kahn-TAHN-teh, ehl ahk-TOHR, lah ahk-TREES.*

Newspapers/*Periódicos*

792. Classified Ads. Los anuncios clasificados.
lohs ah-NOON-see-ohs klah-see-fee-KAH-dohs.

99

SHOPPING & PERSONAL SERVICES

793. Crossword puzzle. El crucigrama.
ehl kroo-see-GRAH-mah.

794. Celebrity news. Las noticias de farándula.
lahs noh-TEE-see-ahs deh fah-RAHN-doo-lah.

795. Front page. La primera plana.
la pree-MEH-rah PLAH-nah.

796. Weather forecast. El pronóstico del tiempo.
ehl proh-NOHS-tee-koh dehl tee-EHM-poh.

797. Report. El reportaje. *ehl reh-pohr-TAH-heh.*

798. Society pages. Las páginas de vida social.
lahs PAH-gee-nahs deh BEE-dah soh-SEE-ahl.

Shopping and Personal Services/Las Compras y los Servicios

799. I want to go shopping. Deseo ir de compras.
deh-SEH-oh eer deh KOHM-prahs.

800. Where is there a bakery?
¿Dónde hay una panadería?
DOHN-deh i OO-nah pah-nah-deh-REE-ah?

801. A candy store, a cigar store.
Una dulcería, una cigarrería.   *OO-nah dool-seh-REE-ah, OO-nah see-gah-rreh-REE-ah.*

802. A clothing store, a department store.
Una tienda de ropa, una tienda por departamentos.
OO-nah tee-EHN-tah deh ROH-pah, OO-nah tee-EHN-dah pohr deh-pahr-tah-MEHN-tohs.

Quick & to the Point

To go shopping. Ir de compras. *eer deh COHM-prahs.*

How can I help you? ¿Cómo puedo ayudarle?
KOH-moh PWEH-doh ah-yoo-DAHR-leh?

I'm just looking, thanks. Sólo estoy mirando, gracias.
SOH-loh ehs-TOY mee-RAHN-doh, GRAH-see-ahs.

Anything else? ¿Algo más? *AHL-goh mahs?*

Are there any sales? ¿Hay algunas ofretas?
i ahl-GOO-nahs oh-FERH-tahs?

Do you take credit cards? ¿Aceptan tarjetas de crédito?
ah-SEHP-tahn tahr-HEH-tahs deh KREH-dee-toh?

Could I have a receipt? ¿Podría darme un recibo?
poh-DREE-ah DAHR-meh oon reh-SEE-boh?

---

803. **A drug store, a grocery.**
    Una farmacia, una tienda de comestibles.
    OO-nah fahr-MAH-see-ah, OO-nah tee-EHN-dah deh
    koh-mehs-TEE-blehs.

804. **A hardware store.** Una ferretería.
    OO-nah feh-rreh-teh-REE-ah.

805. **A hat shop, a jewelry store.**
    Una sombrerería, una joyería. OO-nah sohm-breh-
    reh-REE-ah, OO-nah hoh-yeh-REE-ah.

806. **A market, a shoe store.**
    Un mercado, una zapatería.
    OON mehr-KAH-doh, OO-nah sah-pah-teh-REE-ah.

SHOPPING & PERSONAL SERVICES

807. A tailor shop.   Una sastrería.
OO-nah sahs-treh-REE-ah.

808. Shoe (watch) repairs.
Reparación de zapatos (de reloj).   reh-pah-rah-see-
OHN deh sah-PAH-tohs (deh reh-LOH).
Also see CLOTHING, p._____, and COMMON
OBJECTS p._____.

809. Sale, bargain sale.   Una venta, una ganga.
OO-nah BEHN-tah, OO-nah GAHN-gah.

810. I want to buy _____.   Quiero comprar _____.
kee-EH-roh kohm-PRAHR.

811. I (don't) like this.   (No) me gusta esto.
(noh) meh GOOS-tah EHS-toh.

812. How much is that?   ¿Cuánto cuesta eso?
KWAHN-toh KWEHS-tah EHS-toh?

813. I prefer something better (cheaper).
Prefiero algo mejor (más barato).   preh-fee-EH-roh
AHL-goh meh-HOHR (mahs bah-RAH-toh)

814. Please show me some samples.
Por favor muéstreme unas muestras.   pohr fah-
BOHR moo-EHS-treh-meh OO-nahs moo-EHS-trahs.

815. It is too large (small).   Es muy grande (pequeño).
ehs moo-ee GRAHN-deh (peh-KEE-nyoh).

816. Show me some others.   Muéstreme otros.
moo-EHS-treh-meh OH-trohs.

817. It does not fit.   No me queda bien.
noh meh KEH-dah bee-EHN.

818. Can I order one?   ¿Puedo pedir uno?
PWEH-doh peh-DEER OO-noh?

819. How long will it take?   ¿Cuánto tardará?
KWAHN-toh tahr-dah-RAH?

820. Please take my measurements.
Por favor tome mis medidas.
pohr fah-BOHR TOH-meh mees meh-DEE-dahs.

821. May I try this on?   ¿Me permite probarme esto?
meh-pehr-MEE-teh proh-BAHR-meh EHS-toh?

822. Will you wrap this, please?
¿Por favor, envuelva esto?
pohr fah-BOHR, ehn-BWEL-bah EHS-toh?

823. It doesn't look good on me.   No me queda bien.
noh meh KEH-dah bee-EHN.

824. Whom do I pay?   ¿A quién pago?
ah kee-EHN PAH-goh?

825. Pack this for shipment to _____.
Empaque esto para embarcar a _____.
ehm-PAH-keh EHS-toh PAH-rah ehm-bahr-KAHR ah
_____.

Post Office/Correo

826. Stamp.   El sello, la estampilla, el timbre.
ehl SEH-lyoh, lah ehs-tahm-PEE-yah, ehl TEEM-breh.

827. Envelope.   El sobre.   *ehl SOH-breh.*

Words that Express Surprise or Dissatisfaction

¡Anda!	Good heavens!	**¡Hala!**	Wow!
¡Caramba!	Oh my!	**¡Guay!**	Cool!
¡Puf!	Yuck!	**¡Puag!**	Yucky! (taste)
¡Pírate!	Get lost!	**¡Caray!**	My goodness!
¡Mierda!	Shit!	**¡Maldito!**	Damn!
¡Díos mío!	My God!	**¡Burro!**	Jerk!

828. How much is postage to the United States?
¿Cuánto es de envío a los Estados Unidos?
KWAHN-toh ehs deh ehn-VEE-oh ah lohs ehs-TAH-dos oo-NEE-dohs?

829. A post card (a letter) to _____.
Una tarjeta postal (una carta) para _____.
OO-nah tahr-HEH-tah pohs-TAHL (OO-nah KAHR-tah) PAH-rah _____.

830. I want five _____-cent stamps.
Deseo cinco estampillas (sellos, timbres) de _____ centavos. *deh-SEH-oh SEEN-koh ehs-tahm-PEE-yahs. (SEH-yohs, TEEM-brehs) de _____ sehn-TAH-bohs.*

831. How many stamps do I need?
¿Cuántas estampillas (sellos, timbres) necesito?
KWAHN-tohs ehs-tahm-PEE-yahs (SEH-yohs, TEEM-brehs) neh-seh-SEE-toh?

832. There is nothing subject to duty in this.
No hay nada sujeto a impuesto en esto.
noh i NAH-dah soo-HEH-toh ah eem-PWEHS-toh ehn EHS-toh.

833. Will this go out today? ¿Saldrá esto hoy?
sahl-DRAH EHS-toh oy?

834. Give me a receipt, please.
Déme un recibo, por favor.
DEH-meh oon reh-SEE-boh, pohr fah-BOHR.

835. I want to send a money order.
Quiero mandar un giro postal.
kee-EH-roh mahn-DAHR oon HEE-roh pohs-TAHL.

836. To which window do I go? ¿A qué ventanilla voy?
ah keh behn-tah-NEE-yah boy?

837. By air mail, by parcel post.
Por correo aéreo, por paquete postal. *pohr koh-RREH-oh ah-EH-reh-oh, pohr pah-KEH-teh pohs-TAHL.*

838. Fragile. Frágil. *FRAH-heel.*

839. Registered, special delivery.
Certificado, entrega inmediata. *sehr-tee-fee-KAH-doh, ehn-TREH-gah een-meh-dee-AH-tah.*

840. Insured. Asegurado. *ah-seh-goo-RAH-do.*

841. Mailbox. El buzón. *ehl boo-SOHN.*

Bank/*Banco*

842. When is the bank open?
¿Cuándo se abre el banco?
KWAHN-doh seh AH-breh ehl BAHN-coh?

843. Does the bank have an ATM?
¿Tiene el banco un cajero automático?
tee-EHN-eh ehl BAHN-coh oon kah-HEHR-oh aw-toh MAH-tee-coh?

844. Where is the nearest bank?
¿Dónde está el banco más cercano?   *DOHN-deh ehs-TAH ehl BAHN-koh mahs sehr-KAH-noh?*

845. At which window do I cash this?
¿En qué ventanilla puedo cobrar esto?   *ehn keh behn-tah-NEE-yah PWEH-doh koh-BRAHR EHS-toh?*

846. Can you exchange dollars for euros?
¿Me puede cambiar dólares por euros?
meh PWEH-deh kahm-bee-AHR DOH-lah-rehs pohr EH-oo-rohs.

847. Coins, cents (for euros).   Monedas, centavos.
moh-NEH-dahs, sehn-TAH-bohs.

848. What is the exchange rate on the dollar?
¿A cómo está el cambio del dólar?   *ah KOH-moh ehs-TAH ehl KAHM-bee-oh dehl DOH-lahr?*

849. Can you change this for me?
¿Puede usted cambiarme esto?
PWEH-deh oos-TEHD kahm-bee-AHR-meh EHS-toh?

Note that the date is written in this order: day/
month/year, (not month/day/year as it is done in the
U.S.) Also note that commas are used where we use
decimal points and decimal points are used where
we ordinarily use commas. So five dollars and fifty
cents would be written 5,50 and five thousand would
be written 5.000.

850. Will you cash a check?
¿Quiere usted cobrarme un cheque?   *kee-EH-reh
oos-TEHD koh-BRAHR-meh oon CHEH-keh?*

851. Do not give me large bills, please.
Por favor no me dé billetes grandes.   *pohr-fah-
BOHR, noh meh deh bee-YEHT-tehs GRAHN-dehs.*

852. May I have small change?
¿Puede usted darme cambio?
PWEH-deh oos-TEHD DAR-meh KAHM-bee-oh?

853. Travelers' checks.   Cheques para viajeros.
CHEH-kehs PAH-rah bee-ah-HEH-rohs.

Electronics and Email/*Electrónicos y Correo Electrónico*

854. What is your email address?
¿Cuál es tu dirección de correo electrónico?
*kwal ehs too dee-rehk-see-OHN deh koh-RREH-oh
eh-lehk-TROH-nee-koh?*

855. Can I use this computer to check my email?
¿Puedo usar esta computadora para verificar mi correo electrónico? *PWEH-doh oo-SAHR EHS-tah kohm-poo-tah-DOH-rah PAH-rah beh-ree-fee-KAHR mee koh-RREH-oh eh-lehk-TROH-nee-koh?*

856. Is there an Internet café nearby?
¿Hay un café de internet cerca? *i oon kah-FEH deh een-tehr-NEHT-sehr-KAH?*

857. How much for ten minutes?
¿Cuánto por diez minutos? *KWAHN-toh pohr dee-EHS mee-NOO-tohs?*

858. How do I start this? ¿Cómo empiezo esto? *KOH-moh ehm-pee-EH-soh EHS-toh?*

859. Could you show me how to send a file?
¿Podría mostrarme como enviar un archivo? *poh-DREE-ah mohs-TRAHR-meh KOH-moh ehn-BEE-ahr oon ahr-CHEE-boh?*

860. How do I print this? ¿Cómo imprimo esto? *KOH-moh eem-PREE-moh EHS-toh?*

861. How do you type @? ¿Cómo se escribe arroba? *KOH-moh seh ehs-KREE-beh ah-RROH-bah?*

862. Inbox. El buzón. *ehl boo-SOHN.*

863. The computer doesn't work.
La computadora no funciona. *lah kohm-poo-tah-DOH-rah noh foon-see-OH-nah.*

Internet Vocabulary/*Vocabulario de Internet*

864. Email. El correo electrónico. *ehl koh-REH-oh eh-lehk-TROH-nee-koh.*

865. Email address. La dirección de correo. *lah dee-rehk-see-OHN deh koh-REH-oh.*

866. Website. La página de la red. *lah PAH-hee-nah deh lah rehd.*

867. Internet. El Internet. *ehl EEN-tehr-neht.*

868. Search engine. El motor de búsqueda. *ehl moh-TOHR deh BOOS-keh-dah*

869. Surf the web. Navegar la red. *nah-beh-GAHR lah rehd.*

870. Download. Bajar. *bah-HAHR.*

871. @ Arroba. *ah-RROH-bah.*

872. Dot. Punto. *POON-toh.*

873. Underscore. Subraya. *soob-RAH-yah.*

874. Wi-Fi. Wi-Fi. *wee-fee.*

875. Delete. Borrar. *boh-RRAHR.*

876. File. El fichero/archivo. *ehl fee-CHEH-roh/ahr-CHEE-boh.*

877. Message. El mensaje. *ehl mehn-SAH-heh.*

878. Open. Abrir. *ah-BREER.*

879. Print. Imprimir. *eem-pree-MEER.*

880. Reply. Responder. *rehs-pohn-DEHR.*

Quick & to the Point

an attachment. un archivo adjunto.
oon ahr-CHEE-boh ahd-HOON-toh.

back, forward. atrás, adelante.
ah-TRAHS, ah-deh-LAHN-teh.

a bookmark. un favorito.
oon fah-boh-REE-toh.

chat room. el chat.
ehl chaht.

cut and paste. cortar y pegar.
kohr-TAHR ee PEH-gahr.

delete. borrar.
boh-RAHR.

download. descargar.
dehs-kahr-GAHR.

a file. un archivo.
oon ahr-chee-boh.

flash drive. la memoria instantánea.
lah meh-MOH-ree-ah een-stahn-THA-nee-ah.

folder. la carpeta.
lah karh-PEH-tah.

home. el inicio.
ehl ee-NEE-see-oh.

link. un enlace.
oon ehn-LAH-seh.

the Net. la Red.
lah rehd.

to save as. guardar como.
gwahr-DAHR KOM-oh.

the screen. la pantalla.
lah pahn-TAH-yah.

screensaver. un salvapantallas.
oon sahl-bah-pahn-TAH-yahs.

search engine. un buscador.
oon boos-kah-DOHR.

to search. buscar.
boos-KAHR.

subject. asunto.
ah-SOON-toh.

a text message. un SMS.
oon ehseh-emeh-ehseh.

website. un sitio web.
oon SEE-tee-oh wehb.

Internet cafés are widely available in most cities in Spain and Central and South America. Hotels often offer computers for the use of their guests.

881. Save. Guardar. *gwahr-DAHR.*

882. Is there Internet access here? ¿Hay acceso a internet aquí? *i ahk-SEH-soh ah een-tehr-NEHT ah-KEE?*

883. Chat room. La sala de chat. *lah SAH-lah deh chaht.*

ATMs/ *Cajero Automático*

884. Debit card. La tarjeta de cobro automático. *lah tahr-HEH-tah deh KOH-broh ahw-toh-MAH-tee-koh.*

885. PIN. La clave secreta. *lah KLAH-beh seh-KREH-tah.*

886. My ATM card has been demagnetized. Mi tarjeta del cajero automático ha sido desmagnetizada. *me tahr-HEH-tah dehl kah-HEH-roh ahw-toh-MAH-tee-koh ah SEE-doh deh-mahg-nee-tee-SAH-dah.*

Quick & to the Point

Insert your card. Inserte su tarjeta. *een-SEHR-teh soo tahr-HEH-tah.*

PIN number. El código secreto. *ehl KOH-dee-goh seh-KREH-toh.*

Account. La cuenta. *lah KWEHN-tah.*

887. My card has been stolen.   Mi tarjeta ha sido robada.   *mee tahr-HEH-tah ah SEE-doh roh-BAH-dah.*

888. My card has been eaten by the machine.
Mi tarjeta ha sido tragada por el cajero.
mee tahr-HEH-tah ah SEE-dah trah-GAH-dah pohr ehl kah-HEH-roh.

889. Please enter your PIN.
Por favor, ingrese su clave secreta.   *pohr fah-BOHR, een-GREH-seh soo KLAH-beh seh-KREH-tah.*

890. Please choose your transaction.
Por favor, escoja su transacción.   *pohr fah-BOHR, ehs-KOH-hah soo trahn-sahk-see-OHN.*

891. Balance.   El saldo.   *ehl SAHL-doh.*

892. Withdrawal.   El retiro.   *ehl reh-TEE-roh.*

893. Deposit.   El depósito.   *ehl deh-POH-see-toh.*

894. Transfer.   La transferencia.   *lah trahns-feh-rehn-SEE-ah.*

895. Please choose an account.
Por favor, escoja una cuenta.
pohr fah-BOHR, ehs-KOH-hah OO-nah KWEHN-tah.

896. Checking account.   La cuenta corriente.
lah KWEHN-tah koh-rree-EHN-teh.

897. Savings.   Los ahorros.   *lohs ah-OH-rohs.*

898. Please choose a quantity.
Por favor, escoja una cantidad.   *poh fah-BOHR, ehs-KOH-hah OO-nah kahn-tee-DAHD.*

112

ATMs are widely available in most cities and many towns of the Spanish-speaking world. They are a quick and easy way to withdraw local currency. They often have a very good exchange rate. Use the same caution that you would at an automatic teller at home.

899. Do you want a receipt? ¿Desea un recibo?
deh-SEH-ah oon reh-SEE-boh?

900. Withdraw money. Sacar dinero.
sah-KAHR dee-NEH-roh.

901. Take your receipt and your money.
Recoja su recibo y su dinero.
reh-KOH-hah soo reh-SEE-boh ee soo dee-NEH-roh.

902. Don't forget your card when you finish.
No olvide su tarjeta cuando termine. *noh ohl-BEE-deh soo tahr-HEH-tah KWAHN-doh tehr-MEE-neh.*

903. Cash. Dinero en efectivo.
dee-NEH-roh ehn eh-fehk-TEE-boh.

Bookstores and Office Supply Store/ Librería y Papelería

904. Where is there a bookstore? ¿Dónde hay una librería? *DOHN-deh i OO-nah lee-breh-REE-ah?*

905. Office supply store, a newsstand.
Una papelería, un kiosco.
OO-nah pah-peh-leh-REE-ah, oon kee-OHS-koh.

Quick & to the Point

book. el libro. *ehl LEE-broh.*

magazine. la revista. *lah reh-BEE-stah.*

fiction. ficción. *feek-see-OHN.*

nonfiction. no ficción. *noh feek-see-OHN.*

newspaper. el periódico. *ehl pehr-ee-OH-dee-koh.*

paper. el papel. *ehl pah-PEHL.*

---

906. Newspapers, magazines. Los periódicos, las revistas. *lohs peh-ree-OH-dee-kohs, lahs reh-BEES-tahs.*

907. A dictionary, a guidebook. Un diccionario, una guía. *oon deek-see-oh-NAH-ree-oh, OO-nah GEE-ah.*

908. A map of _____. Un mapa de _____. *oon MAH-pah deh _____.*

909. Playing cards, post cards. Los naipes, las tarjetas postales. *lohs NI-pehs, lahs tahr-HEH-tahs pohs-TAH-lehs.*

910. Greeting cards. Las tarjetas de felicitación. *lahs tahr-HEH-tahs deh feh-lee-see-tah-see-OHN.*

911. Writing paper, ink. El papel para cartas, la tinta. *ehl pah-PEHL PAH-rah KAHR-tahs, lah TEEN-tah.*

912. Envelopes, pencil. Los sobres, el lápiz. *lohs SOH-brehs, ehl LAH-pees.*

913. A pen, artist's materials.

Un bolígrafo, los materiales para pintores.
*oon boh-LEE-grah-foh, lohs mah-teh-ree-AH-lehs
PAH-rah peen-TOH-rehs.*

914. (Strong) string, an eraser.

La cuerda (fuerte), el borrador.
lah KWEHR-dah (FWEHR-teh), ehl boh-rrah-DOHR.

Pens

This is another word that varies from one country to another.

pen can be:

pluma	*ploo-mah* or	
lapicera	*lah-pee-SEHR-ah*	in Argentina, Uruguay and Chile
lapicero	*lah-pee-SEHR-oh*	in Peru
bolígrafo	*boh-LEE-grah-foh*	in Spain

A ballpoint pen can be:

bolígrafo	*boh-LEE-grah-foh* or	
punta bola	*POONT-ah BOHL-ah*	in Bolivia
lapicera de pasta	*lah-pee-SEHR-ah deh PAHS-tah*	in Chile
esfero	*ehs-FEHR-oh*	in Colombia

---

915. Tissue paper, wrapping paper.
El papel de seda, el papel para envolver.
ehl pah-PEHL deh SEH-dah, ehl pah-PEHL PAH-rah ehn-bohl-BEHR.

Cigar Store/Tabaquería

916. Where is the nearest cigar store?
¿Dónde está la tabaquería más cercana?
DOHN-deh ehs-TAH lah tah-bah-keh-REE-ah mahs-sehr-KAH-nah?

917. I want some cigars. Deseo unos cigarros or puros.
deh-SEH-oh OO-nohs see-GAH-rrohs or POO-rohs.

918. A pack of cigarettes, please.
Un paquete de cigarillos, por favor. *oon pah-KEH-teh deh see-gah-REE-yohs, pohr fah-BOHR.*

919. I need a lighter. Necesito un encendedor.
neh-seh-SEE-toh oon ehn-sehn-deh-DOHR.

920. Matches, a pipe. Los fósforos, una pipa.
lohs FOHS-foh-rohs, OO-nah PEE-pah.

921. Pipe tobacco, a pouch.
El tabaco, una bolsa para tabaco. *ehl tah-BAH-koh, OO-nah BOHL-sah PAH-rah tah-BAH-koh.*

Barber Shop and Hair Salon/Peluquería y Salón de Belleza

922. Where is there a good barber?
¿Dónde hay un buen peluquero?
DOHN-deh i oon bwehn peh-loo KEH-roh?

Quick & to the Point

shave.	una afeitada.	*OO-nah ah-fay-TAH-tah.*
haircut.	un corte de pelo.	*oon KOHR-teh deh PEH-loh.*
manicure.	una manicura.	*OO-nah mahn-ee-COOR-ah.*

923. I want a haircut (shave).
Quisiera que me cortara el pelo (una afeitada).
*kee-see-EH-rah keh meh kohr-TAH-rah ehl PEH-loh
(OO-nah ah-fay-TAH-dah).*

924. Not very short.   No muy corto.
noh moo-ee KOHR-toh.

925. Do not cut any off the top.
No corte nada de arriba.
noh KOHR-teh NAH-dah deh ah-REE-bah.

926. At the back and sides.   De atrás y de los lados.
deh ah-TRAHS ee deh lohs LAH-dohs.

927. I part my hair on the (other) side.
Me hago la raya al (otro) lado.
meh AH-goh lah RAH-yah ahl (OH-troh) LAH-doh.

928. In the middle.   En el medio.   *ehn ehl MEH-dee-oh.*

929. The water is too hot (cold).
El agua está muy caliente (fría).   *ehl AH-gwah ehs-
TAH mwee kah-lee-EHN-teh (FREE-ah).*

930. Can I make an appointment for _____?
¿Puedo hacer una cita para _____?   *PWEH-doh
ah-SEHR OO-nah SEE-tah PAH-rah _____?*

There isn't a separate word for toenails in Spanish. Fingernails are *uñas* (OO-nyahs) and toenails are *uñas de pie* (OO-nyahs deh PEE-eh) or nails of the foot!

931. I would like a shampoo and set.

Me gustaría un champú y peinado.   *meh goos-tah-REE-ah oon chahm-POO ee peh-ee-NAH-doh.*

932. A perm.   Un permanente.   *oon pehr-mah-NEHN-teh.*

933. A facial, a manicure.   Un facial, una manicura.
oon fah-see-AHL , OO-nah mah-nee-KOO-rah.

934. Nail polish.   Esmalte de uñas.
ehs-MAHL-teh deh OO-nyahs.

935. A pedicure.   Una pedicura.
OO-nah peh-dee-KOO-rah.

936. Wax my eyebrows, lips, chin.

Quiero que me depile las cejas, el labio, la barbilla.
kee-YEH-roh keh meh deh-PEE-leh lahs SEH-hahs, ehl LAH-bee-oh, lah bahr-BEE-yah.

Photography/*Fotografía*

937. I need a memory card.

Necesito un tarjeta de memoria.   *neh-seh-SEE-toh OO-nah tahr-HEH-tah deh meh-MOH-ree-ah.*

Quick & to the Point

camera. la cámara. *lah KAHM-mah-rah.*

memory card. la tarjeta de memoria.
lah tahr-HEH-tah deh me-MOHR-ee-ah.

batteries. las baterías. *lahs bah-teh-REE-ahs.*

938. I want to print some photos.
Quiero imprimir algunas fotografías.   *kee-EH-roh
eem-pree-MEER ahl-GOO-nahs foh-toh-grah-FEE-ahs.*

939. How much do_____ prints cost?
¿Cuánto cuesta revelar_____ fotos?   *KWAHN-toh
KWEHS-tah reh-beh-LAHR _____ FOH-tohs?*

940. An enlargement.   Una ampliación.
OO-nah ahm-plee-ah-see-OHN.

941. My camera isn't working.
Mi cámara está descompuesta.
mee KAH-mah-rah ehs-TAH dehs-kohm-PWEHS-tah.

942. When will they be ready?
¿Cuándo estarán listas?
KWAN-doh ehs-tah-RAHN LEES-tahs?

943. Do you rent cameras?   ¿Se alquilan cámaras?
seh ahl-KEE-lahn KAH-mah-rahs?

944. I would like one for today.   Quisiera una para hoy.
kee-see-EH-rah OO-nah PAH-rah oy.

119

When people in Spain count on their fingers, they start with the thumb, be careful in indicating you want one of something. Holding up your index finger might be interpreted as two!

945. Do you have batteries for this camera?
¿Tiene pilas por esta cámara?
tee-EH-neh PEE-lahs pohr EHS-tah KAH-mah-rah?

Laundry and Dry Cleaning/*Lavandería y Tintorería*

946. Laundry.   La lavandería.   *lah lah-bahn-deh-REE-ah.*

947. Dry cleaners.   La tintorería.   *lah teen-tohr-eh-REE-ah.*

948. I need them by tomorrow afternoon.
Los necesito para mañana por la tarde.
lohs nehs-eh-SEE-toh PAH-rah mah-NYA-nah pohr lah TAHR-deh.

949. Where is the nearest laundry (dry cleaner)?
¿Dónde está la lavandería (la tintorería) más cercana?
DOHN-deh ehs-TAH lah lah-bahn-deh-REE-ah (lah teen-toh-reh-REE-ah) mahs sehr-KAH-nah?

950. I have something to be washed.
Tengo algo para lavar.   *TEHN-goh AHL-goh PAH-rah lah-VAHR.*

951. Pressed (mended).   Para planchar (remendar).
PAH-rah plahn-CHAHR (reh-mehn-DAHR).

952. For the dry cleaner.   Para la tintorería.
PAH-rah lah teen-toh-reh-REE-ah.

953. Don't wash this in hot water.
No lave esto en agua caliente.
noh LAH-beh EHS-toh ehn AH-gwah kah-lee-EHN-teh.

954. Use lukewarm water.   Use agua tibia.
OO-seh AH-gwah tee-BEE-ah.

955. Be very careful.   Tenga mucha cuidado.
TEHN-gah MOO-chah kwee-DAH-doh.

956. Do not starch the collars.   No almidone los cuellos.
noh ahl-mee-DOH-neh lohs KWEH-yohs.

957. When can I have this?   ¿Cuándo puedo tener esto?
KWAHN-doh PWEH-doh teh-NEHR EHS-toh?

958. Here is the list.   Aquí tiene usted la lista.
ah-KEE tee-EH-neh oos-TEHD la LEES-tah.

959. The belt is missing.   Falta el cinturón.
FAHL-tah ehl seen-too-ROHN.

Clothing/Vestidos

960. Apron, bathing cap.   El delantal, el gorro de baño.
ehl deh-lahn-TAHL, ehl GOH-rroh deh BAH-nyoh.

961. Bathing suit, blouse.   El traje de baño, la blusa.
ehl TRAH-heh deh BAH-nyoh, lah BLOO-sah.

962. Bra, coat.   El sostén, el abrigo.   *ehl sohs-TEHN, ehl ah-BREE-goh.*

963. Collar, diapers.   El cuello, los pañales.
ehl KWEH-yoh, lohs pah-NYAH-lehs.

121

Quick & to the Point

How much is it? ¿Cuánto cuesta? *KWAHN-toh KWEHS-tah?*

What size do you want? ¿Qué talla usa? *keh TAH-yah OO-sah?*

I would like a larger (smaller) size.
Me gustaría una talla más grande (pequeña). *meh goos-tah-REE-ah OO-nah TAH-yah mahs GRAHN-deh (peh-KEH-nyoh)?*

What size shoe do you wear? ¿Qué número calzas? *keh NOO-meh-roh CAHL-sahs?*

Can I look at the striped T-shirt?
¿Puedo mirar la camiseta rayada? *pweh-do MEE-rahr lah kah-mee-SEH-tah rah-YAH-dah?*

I'll take it. Me lo llevo. *meh loh YEH-boh.*

---

964. Dress. El vestido. *ehl behs-TEE-doh.*

965. Gloves, handkerchief. Los guantes, el pañuelo. *lohs GWAHN-tehs, ehl pah-nyoo-EH-loh.*

966. Hat, jacket. El sombrero, la chaqueta. *ehl sohm-BREH-roh, lah chah-KEH-tah.*

967. Necktie, nightgown. La corbata, el camisón. *lah kohr-BAH-tah, ehl kah-mee-SOHN.*

968. Overcoat, pajamas. El abrigo, el pijama. *ehl ah-BREE-goh, ehl pee-HAH-mah.*

969. Panties. Las bragas. *lahs BRAH-gahs.*

970. Robe, shirt. La bata, la camisa. *lah BAH-tah, lah kah-MEE-sah.*

971. Raincoat, shorts. El impermeable, los pantalones cortos. *ehl eem-pehr-mee-AH-bleh, lohs pahn-tah-LOH-nehs KOHR-tohs.*

972. Shorts (men's underwear), skirt. Los calzoncillos, la falda. *lohs kahl-sohn-SEE-yohs, lah FAHL-dah.*

973. Slip, slippers. La combinación, las zapatillas. *lah kohm-bee-nah-see-OHN, lahs sah-pah-TEE-yahs.*

974. Socks, stockings. Los calcetines, las medias. *lohs kahl-seh-TEE-nehs, lahs MEH-dee-ahs.*

975. Suit, suspenders. El traje, los tirantes. *ehl TRAH-heh, lohs tee-RAHN-tehs.*

976. Sweater, trousers. El suéter, los pantalones. *ehl SWEH-tehr, lohs pahn-tah-LOH-nehs.*

977. Undershirt, underwear. La camiseta, la ropa interior. *lah kah-mee-SEH-tah, lah ROH-pah een-teh-ree-OHR.*

978. Vest. El chaleco. *ehl chah-LEH-koh.*

979. Size small (medium, large). Tamaño pequeño (mediano, grande). *tah-MAH-nyoh peh-KEH-nyoh (meh-dee-AH-noh, GRAHN-deh).*

When traveling to other countries, it's a good idea to look up size conversion charts for men, women, and children. Shoe sizes are also measured differently in various countries, so be prepared with the appropriate conversions for the sizes.

Health/*Salud*

Accidents/Accidentes

980. There has been an accident. Hubo un accidente. *OO-boh oon ahk-see-DEHN-teh.*

981. Get a doctor (nurse). Llame a un doctor, una doctora (un enfermero, una enfermera). *YAH-meh a oon dohk-TOHR , OO-nah dohk-TOH-rah (oon ehn-fehr-MEH-roh, OO-nah ehn-fehr-MEH-rah).*

982. I need help. Necesito ayuda. *neh-seh-SEE-toh ah-YOO-dah.*

983. Help! ¡Socorro! ¡Auxillio! *soh-KOH-rroh! ahw-SEE-lee-oh!*

984. Send for an ambulance. Mande a buscar una ambulancia. *MAHN-deh ah BOOS-kahr OO-nah ahm-boo-LAHN-see-ah.*

Quick & to the Point

Help! ¡Socorro! *soh-KOH-rroh!*

I need a policeman. Necesito un policía.
neh-seh-SEE-toh oon poh-lee-SEE-ah.

Call an ambulance. Llame a una ambulancia.
YAH-meh ah OO-nah ahm-boo-LAHN-see-ah.

Does anyone have a cell phone? ¿Tiene alguien un móvil?
tee-EH-neh ahl-GEE-ehn oon MOH-beel?

985. Please bring blankets.
  Por favor, traiga unas mantas (cobijas). *pohr fah-BOHR, TRI-gah OO-nahs MAHN-tahs (koh-BEE-hahs).*

986. A stretcher, water. Una camilla, agua.
  OO-nah kah-MEE-yah, AH-gwah.

987. He is (seriously) hurt. Está (gravemente) herido.
  ehs-TAH-(grah-beh-MEHN-teh) eh-REE-doh.

988. Help me carry him (her).
  Ayúdeme a cargarlo (cargarla). *ah-YOO-deh-meh ah kahr-GAHR-loh (cahr-GAHR-lah).*

989. He was knocked down. Fué atropellado.
  fweh ah-troh-peh-YAH-doh.

990. She has fallen (fainted). Ella se cayó (se desmayó).
  EH-yah seh kah-YOH (seh dehs-mah-YOH).

991. I feel faint. Estoy mareado.
  ehs-TOY mah-reh-AH-doh.

992. He has a fracture (bruise, cut).
  Tiene una fractura (una contusión, un corte). *tee-EH-neh OO-nah frahk-TOO-rah (OO-nah kohn-too-see-OHN, oon KOHR-teh).*

993. He has burned his hand. Se quemó la mano.
  seh keh-MOH lah MAH-noh.

994. It is bleeding (swollen). Está sangrando (hinchado).
  ehs-TAH sahn-GRAHN-doh (een-CHAH-doh).

995. Can you dress this? ¿Puede usted curar esto?
  PWEH-deh oos-TEHD koo-RAHR EHS-toh?

996. Do you have any bandages (a splint)?
¿Tiene vendas (una tablilla)?
tee-EH-neh BEHN-dahs (OO-nah tah-BLEE-yah)?

997. I need something for a tourniquet.
Necesito algo para un torniquete.   *neh-seh-SEE-toh*
AHL-goh PAH-rah oon tohr-nee-KEH-teh.

998. Are you all right?   ¿Está usted bien?
ehs-TAH oos-TEHD bee-EHN?

999. It hurts here.   Me duele aquí.
meh DWEH-leh ah-KEE.

1000. I want to sit down a moment.
Quiero sentarme un momento.
kee-EH-roh sehn TAHR-meh oon moh-MEHN-toh.

1001. I can't move my _____.
No puedo mover mi _____.
noh PWEH-doh moh-BEHR mee _____.

1002. I have hurt my _____.   Me lastimé el _____.
meh lahs-tee-MEH ehl _____.

1003. Can I travel on Monday?   ¿Puedo viajar el lunes?
PWEH-doh bee-ah-HAHR ehl LOO-nehs?

1004. Please notify my husband (wife).
Por favor avísele a mi esposo (esposa).
pohr fah-BOHR ah-BEE-seh-leh ah mee ehs-POH-soh
(ehs-POH-sah).

1005. Here is my identification.
Aquí tiene mi carnet de identificación.
ah-KEE tee-EH-neh mee kahr-NEHT deh ee-dehn-tee-
fee-kah-see-OHN.

Alternative Treatments

aromatherapy. la aromaterapia.
lah ah-roh-mah-tehr-AH-pee-ah.

herbalist. el herborista. *ehl ehr-bohr-EES-tah.*

homeopathy. la homeopatía.
lah ohm-ee-oh-pah-TEE-ah.

massage. el masaje. *ehl mah-SAH-heh.*

massage therapist. la masajista.
lah mah-sah-HEES-tah.

meditation. la meditación.
lah meh-dee-tah-see-OHN.

naturopath. el naturópata.
ehl nah-toor-OH-pah-tah.

reflexology. la reflexología.
lah reh-fleks-oh-loh-HEE-ah.

yoga. el yoga. *ehl YOH-gah.*

Parts and Organs of the Body/*Partes y Órganos del Cuerpo*

1006. The ankle. El tobillo. *ehl toh-BEE-yo.*

1007. The appendix. El apéndice. *ehl ah-PEN-dee-seh.*

1008. The arm. El brazo. *ehl BRAH-soh.*

1009. The back. La espalda. *lah ehs-PAHL-dah.*

1010. The blood. La sangre. *lah SAHN-greh.*

1011. The bone. El hueso. *ehl WEH-so.*

1012. The cheek. La mejilla. *lah meh-HEE-yah.*

1013. The chest. El pecho. *ehl PEH-choh.*

1014. The chin. La barba. *lah BAHR-bah.*

1015. The collarbone. La clavícula. *lah klah-BEE-koo-lah.*

1016. The ear. La oreja. *lah oh-REH-jah.*

1017. The elbow. El codo. *ehl COH-doh.*

1018. The eye. El ojo. *ehl OH-hoh.*

1019. The eyebrow. La ceja. *lah SEH-hah.*

1020. The eyelash. La pestaña. *lah pehs-TAH-nyah.*

1021. The eyelid. El párpado. *ehl PAHR-pah-doh.*

1022. The face. La cara. *lah KAH-rah.*

1023. The finger. El dedo. *ehl DEH-doh.*

1024. The foot. El pie. *ehl pee-EH.*

1025. The forehead. La frente. *lah FREHN-teh.*

1026. The hair. El pelo. *ehl PEH-loh.*

1027. The hand. La mano. *la MAH-noh.*

1028. The head. La cabeza. *lah kah-BEH-sah.*

1029. The heart. El corazón. *ehl koh-rah-SOHN.*

1030. The heel. El talón. *ehl tah-LOHN.*

1031. The hip. La cadera. *lah kah-DEH-rah.*

1032. The intestines. Los intestinos. *lohs een-tehs-TEE-nohs.*

1033. The jaw. La mandíbula. *lah mahn-DEE-boo-lah.*

1034. The joint. La coyuntura. *lah koh-yoon-TOO-rah.*

1035. The kidney. El riñón. *ehl rree-NYOHN.*

1036. The knee. La rodilla. *lah rroh-DEE-yah.*

1037. The leg. La pierna. *lah pee-EHR-nah.*

1038. The lip. El labio. *ehl LAH-bee-oh.*

1039. The liver. El hígado. *ehl EE-gah-doh.*

1040. The lung. El pulmón. *ehl pool-MOHN.*

1041. The mouth. La boca. *lah BOH-kah.*

1042. The muscle. El músculo. *ehl MOOS-koo-loh.*

1043. The nail (finger, toe). La uña. *lah OO-nyah.*

1044. The neck. El cuello. *ehl KWEH-yoh.*

1045. The nerve. El nervio. *ehl NEHR-vee-oh.*

1046. The nose. La nariz. *lah nah-REES.*

1047. The rib. La costilla. *lah kohs-TEE-yah.*

1048. The shoulder. El hombro. *ehl OHM-broh.*

1049. The (left, right) side.
El costado (izquierdo, derecho).
ehl kohs-TAH-doh (ees-kee-EHR-doh, deh-REH-choh).

1050. The skin. La piel. *lah pee-EHL.*

1051. The skull. El cráneo. *ehl KRAH-neh-oh.*

1052. The spine. La espina. *lah ehs-PEE-nah.*

1053. The stomach. El estómago. *ehl ehs-TOH-mah-goh.*

What they may say to you at the doctor's office:

What's the matter? ¿Qué le pasa?
keh leh PAH-SAH?

Do you feel any pain? ¿Le duele? *leh DWEH-leh?*

Where does it hurt? ¿Dónde le duele?
DOHN-deh leh DWEH-le?

Do you have a fever? ¿Tiene fiebre?
tee-EHN-eh fee-EH-breh?

How long have you had this?
Desde cuándo se siente así?
DEHS-deh KWAHN-doh seh see-EHN-teh ah-SEE?

Are you allergic to any medicine?
¿Es alérgico/a a alguna medicina? *ehs ahl-EHR-hee-
koh/kah ah ahl-GOON-ah meh-dee-CEEN-ah?*

Are you on medication?
¿Se encuentra bajo medicación? *seh ehn-KWEHN-trah
BAH-hoh meh-dee-kah-see-OHN?*

Are you pregnant? ¿Está embarazada?
ehs-TAH ehm-bahr-ah-SAH-dah?

cold. resfriado. *rehs-free-AH-doh.*

cough. tos. *tohs.*

fever. fiebre. *fee-EH-breh.*

sore throat. dolor de garganta.
doh-lohr deh gahr-gahn-tah.

vomiting. vomitar. *bohm-ee-TAHR.*

1054. The tooth.   El diente.   *el dee-EHN-teh.*

1055. The tendon.   El tendón   *ehl ten-DOHN.*

1056. The thigh.   El muslo.   *ehl MOOS-loh.*

1057. The throat.   La garganta.   *lah gahr-GAHN-tah.*

1058. The thumb.   El pulgar.   *ehl pool-GAHR.*

1059. The toe.   El dedo del pie.   *ehl DEH-doh dehl PEE-eh.*

1060. The tongue.   La lengua.   *lah LEHN-gwah.*

1061. The tonsils.   Las amígdalas.   *lahs ah-MEHG-dah-lahs.*

1062. The waist.   La cintura.   *lah sehn-TOO-rah.*

1063. The wrist.   La muñeca.   *lah moo-NYEH-kah.*

Illness/Enfermedad

1064. I want to see a doctor.   Deseo ver a un doctor.
deh-SEH-oh BEHR ah oon dohk-TOHR.

1065. A specialist, an American doctor.
Un especialista, un médico norteamericano.
oon ehs-peh-see-ah-LEES-tah, oon MEH-dee-koh nohr-teh-ah-meh-ree-KAH-noh.

1066. I don't sleep well.   No duermo bien.
noh DWEHR-moh BEE-ehn.

1067. My foot hurts.   Me duele el pie.
meh DWEH-leh ehl pee-EH.

1068. My head aches.   Tengo dolor de cabeza.
TEHN-goh doh-LOHR deh kah-BEH-sah.

Quick & to the Point

I have a fever.   Tengo fiebre.   *TEHN-goh fee-EH-breh.*

I have a cough.   Tengo tos.   *TEHN-goh tohs.*

I am allergic to . . .   Soy alérgico a . . .
SOH-ee ah-LEHR-hee-koh ah . . .

   aspirin.   la aspirina.   *lah ahs-pee-REE-nah.*

   penicillin.   la penicilina.   *lah peh-nee-see-LEE-nah.*

   sulpha drug.   la sulfonamida.   *lah sool-foh-nah-MEE-dah.*

   iodine.   el yodo.   *ehl YOH-doh.*

   novocaine.   la novocaína.   *lah noh-boh-cah-EE-nah.*

   latex.   el latex.   *ehl LAH-tehks.*

It hurts here.   Me duele aquí.   *meh DWEH-leh ah-KEE.*

1069. I have an abscess.   Tengo un absceso.
TEHN-goh oon ahb-SEH-soh.

1070. I have allergies.   Tengo alergias.
TEHN-goh ah-LEHR-hee-ahs.

1071. Appendicitis.   El apendicitis.   *ehl ah-pehn-dee-SEE-tees.*

1072. A bite (insect), a blister.
Una picadura, una ampolla.
OO-nah pee-kah-DOO-rah, OO-nah ahm-POH-yah.

1073. A boil, a burn.   Un divieso, una quemadura.
oon dee-bee-EH-soh, OO-nah keh-mah-DOO-rah.

1074. Chills, a cold.   Los escalofríos, un catarro.
lohs ehs-kah-loh-FREE-ohs, oon kah-TAH-roh.

1075. Constipation, a cough. El estreñimiento, una tos.
ehl ehs-tre-nyee-mee-EHN-toh, OO-nah tohs.

1076. A cramp, diarrhea, dysentery.
Un calambre, la diarrea, la disentería. *oon kah-LAHM-breh, lah dee-ah-RREH-ah, lah dee-sehn-teh-REE-ah.*

1077. Earache, fever. El dolor de oído, la fiebre.
ehl doh-LOHR deh oh-EE-doh, lah fee-EH-breh.

1078. Food poisoning, a headache.
La intoxicación alimentaria, el dolor de cabeza.
lah een-tohk-see-kah-see-OHN ah-lee-mehn-TAHR-ee-ah, ehl doh-LOHR deh kah-BEH-sah.

1079. Hoarseness, indigestion. La ronquera, la indigestión.
lah rohn-KEH-rah, lah een-dee-hehs-tee-OHN.

1080. Nausea, pneumonia. Las náuseas, la pulmonía.
lahs NAW-see-ahs, lah pool-moh-NEE-ah.

1081. A sore throat, a sprain.
Una inflamación de la garganta, una torcedura.
OO-nah een flah-mah-see-OHN deh lah gahr-GAHN-tah, OON-ah tohr-seh-DOO-rah.

1082. A sting, sunburn. Una picadura, una quemadura
del sol. *OO-nah pee-cah-DOO-rah, OO-nah keh-mah-DOO-rah-dehl sohl.*

1083. Sunstroke, typhoid fever, vomiting.
La insolación, la fiebre tifoidea, los vómitos.
lah een-soh-lah-see-OHN, lah fee-EH-breh tee-foh-ee-DEH-ah, lohs BOH-mee-tohs.

1084. What should I do? ¿Qué debo hacer?
keh DEH-boh AH-sehr?

1085. Do I have to stay in bed?
¿Tengo que guardar cama?
TEHN-goh keh gwahr-DAHR KAHM-ah?

1086. Do I have to go to the hospital?
¿Tengo que ir al hospital?
TEHN-goh keh eer-ahl ohs-pee-TAHL?

1087. May I get up? ¿Puedo levantarme?
PWEH-doh leh-bahn-TAHR-meh?

1088. I feel better. Me siento mejor.
meh-see-EHN-toh meh-HOHR.

1089. When do you think I'll be better?
¿Cuándo cree que me sentiré mejor? *KWAHN-doh
KREH-eh keh meh sehn-tee-REH meh-HOHR?*

1090. When will you come again? ¿Cuándo vuelve usted?
KWAHN-doh BWEHL-beh OOS-tehd?

1091. A drop. Una gota. *OO-nah GOH-tah.*

1092. A tablespoonful, a teaspoonful.
Una cucharada, una cucharadita. *OO-nah koo-
chah-RAH-dah, OO-nah koo-chah-rah-DEE-tah.*

1093. Every hour (3 hours). Cada hora (tres horas).
KAH-dah OH-rah (trehs OH-rahs).

1094. Before (after) meals.
Antes (después) de las comidas.
AHN-tehs (dehs-PWEHS) deh lahs koh-MEE-dahs.

1095. Twice a day. Dos veces al día.
dohs BEH-sehs ahl DEE-ah.

1096. At bedtime, when getting up.
Al acostarse, al levantarse.
ahl ah-kohs-TAHR-seh, ahl leh-bahn-TAHR-seh.

1097. X-ray, sonogram. La radiografía, el ultrasonido.
lah rah-dee-oh-grah-FEE-ah, ehl ool-trah-soh-NEE-doh.

1098. MRI, CAT scan.
Resonador Magnético, tac (tomógrafo)
reh-soh-nah-DOHR mahg-NEH-tee-koh, tahk (toh-MOH-grah-foh)

Dentist/Dentista

1099. Where is there a good dentist?
¿Dónde hay un buen dentista?
DOHN-deh i oon bwehn dehn-TEES-tah?

1100. This tooth hurts. Me duele este diente.
meh DWEH-leh EHS-teh dee-EHN-teh.

Quick & to the Point

I have a toothache. Me duele una muela.
meh DWEH-leh OO-nah MWEH-lah.

I have a cavity. Tengo una caries.
TEHN-goh OO-nah kah-REE-ehs.

Please give me an anesthetic. Por favor, póngame anestesia.
pohr fah-BOHR, POHN-gah-meh ahn-ehs-TEES-ee-ah.

Ouch! ¡Ay!

1101. Can you fix it (temporarily)?
¿Puede componerlo (por ahora)?
PWE-deh kohm-poh-NEHR-loh (pohr ah-OH-rah)?

1102. I have lost a filling. Perdí una tapadura.
pehr-DEE OO-nah tah-pah-DOO-rah.

1103. I have broken a tooth. Me rompí un diente.
me rohm-PEE oon dee-EHN-teh.

1104. I do not want it extracted. No deseo que lo saque.
noh deh-SEH-oh keh loh SAH-keh.

1105. Can you repair this denture?
¿Puede componer esta dentadura? *PWEH-deh*
kohm-poh-NEHR EHS-tah dehn-tah-DOO-rah?

1106. Local anesthetic. Un anestético local.
oon ahn-nehs-TEH-tee-koh loh-KAHL.

Drugstore/Farmacia

1107. Where is a drugstore where they speak English?
¿Dónde hay una farmacia donde se hable inglés?
DOHN-deh i OO-nah fahr-MAH-see-ah DOHN-de
seh AH-bleh een-GLEHS?

1108. Can you fill this prescription?
¿Puede prepararme esta receta? *PWEH-deh preh-*
pah-RAHR-meh EHS-tah reh-SEH-tah?

1109. How long will it take? ¿Cuánto tiempo tardará?
KWAHN-toh tee-EHM-poh tahr-da-RAH?

1110. I want adhesive tape. Quiero esparadrapo.
kee-EH-roh ehs-pah-rah-DRAH-poh.

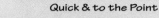

Quick & to the Point

Where is the nearest all-night pharmacy?
¿Dónde está la farmacia de guardia más cercana?
DOHN-deh ehs-TAH lah fahr-MAH-see-ah deh GWAHR-dee-ah mahs sehr-KAHN-ah?

Here is my prescription.   Aquí tiene mi receta médica.
ah-KEE tee-EHN-eh mee reh-SEH-tah MEHD-ee-kah.

Take two tablets three times a day.
Tome dos píldoras tres veces al día.
TOH-meh dohs PEEL-dohr-ahs trehs BEH-sees ahl DEE-ah.

Take after meals.   Tome después de las comidas.
TOH-meh dehs-PWEHS deh lahs koh-MEE-dahs.

I would like an antibiotic.   Me gustaría un antibiótico.
meh goos-tah-REE-ah oon ahn-tee-bee-OH-tee-koh.

May I have an aspirin?   ¿Puedo tener una aspirina?
PWEH-doh tehn-EHR OO-nah ahs-peer-EE-nah?

Do you have contraceptives?   ¿Tienen anticonceptivos?
tee-EHN-ehn ahn-tee-kohn-sehp-TEE-bohs?

I need cough medicine.   Necesito un jarabe para la tos.
neh-seh-SEE-toh oon hah-RAH-beh PAH-rah lah tohs.

Do you have laxatives?   ¿Tiene laxantes?
tee-EHN-eh laks-AHN-tehs?

A painkiller, please.   Un analgésico, por favor.
oon ahn-ahl-HEHS-ee-coh, pohr fah-BOHR.

I would like sleeping pills.   Me gustaría pastillas para dormir.
meh goos-tah-REE-ah pah-STEE-yahs PAH-rah dohr-MEER.

137

1111. Alcohol, analgesic. El alcohol, el analgésico.
ehl ahl-koh-HOHL, ehl ah-nahl-HEHS-see-koh.

1112. An antiseptic, aspirin. Un antiséptico, una aspirina.
oon ahn-tee-sehp-TEE-koh, OO-nah ahs-pee-REE-nah.

1113. Bandages, bicarbonate of soda.
Las vendas, el bicarbonato de soda. *lahs BEHN-dahs, ehl bee-kahr-boh-NAH-toh deh SOH-dah.*

1114. Boric acid. El ácido bórico. *ehl AH-see-doh BOH-ree-coh.*

1115. A brush (hair, tooth), candle. Un cepillo (de pelo, de dientes), una vela. *oon seh-PEE-yoh (deh PEH-loh, deh dee-EHN-tehs), OO-nah BEH-lah.*

1116. Cleaning fluid (stain remover). El quitamanchas.
ehl kee-tah-MAHN-chahs.

1117. Cold cream, a comb. La crema para la cara, un peine. *lah KREH-mah PAH-rah lah KAH-rah, oon PAY-neh.*

1118. Condom. El condón. *ehl kohn-DOHN.*

1119. Corn pads, cotton. Los parches para los callos, el algodón. *lohs PAHR-chehs PAH-rah lohs KAH-yohs, ehl ahl-goh-DOHN.*

1120. A depilatory, a deodorant.
Un depilatorio, un desodorante. *oon deh-pee-lah-TOH-ree-oh, oon deh-soh-doh-RAHN-teh.*

1121. Ear plugs. Los tapones para el oído.
lohs tah-POH-nehs PAH-rah ehl oh-EE-doh.

1122. **Electric shaver, hair dryer.** La maquinilla de afeitar
eléctronica, el secador. *lah mah-kee-NEE-yah deh
ah-fay-TAHR eh-LEHK-troh-nee-kah, ehl seh-kah-DOHR.*

1123. **Epsom salts.** El sulfato de magnesia.
ehl sool-FAH-toh deh mahg-NEH-see-ah.

1124. **Foot powder.** El talco para los pies.
ehl TAHL-koh PAH-rah lohs pee-EHS.

1125. **Gauze, hair spray.** La gasa, la laca para el pelo.
lah GAH-sah, lah LAH-kah PAH-rah ehl PEH-loh.

1126. **A hot water bottle, an ice bag.**
Una bolsa de agua caliente, una bolsa de hielo.
*OO-nah BOHL-sah deh AH-gwah kah-lee-EHN-teh,
OO-nah BOHL-sah deh YEH-loh.*

1127. **Insect bite lotion, insect repellent.** La loción para
picaduras, el insecticida. *lah loh-see-OHN PAH-rah
pee-kah-DOO-rahs, ehl een-sehk-tee-SEE-dah.*

1128. **Iodine, a laxative.** El yodo, un laxante.
ehl YOH-doh, oon lahk-SAHN-teh.

1129. **A lipstick, a medicine dropper.**
Un lápiz de labios, un gotero.
oon LAH-pees deh LAH-bee-ohs, oon goh-TEH-roh.

1130. **A mouthwash.** Un enjuage bucal.
oon ehn-hoo-AH-geh boo-kahl.

1131. **Peroxide, poison.** El agua oxigenada, el veneno.
ehl AH-gwah ohk-seh-heh-NAH-dah, ehl beh-NEE-noh.

1132. **Powder.** Los polvos. *lohs POHL-vohs.*

1133. A razor, razor blades. Una navaja de afeitar, unas hojas de afeitar. *OO-nah nah-BAH-hah deh ah-fay-TAHR, OO-nahs OH-hahs deh ah-fay-TAHR.*

1134. Rouge (Blusher). El colorete. *ehl koh-loh-REHT-teh.*

Contacts and Glasses

glasses. las gafas, los lentes. *lahs GAH-fahs, lohs LEHN-tehs.*

sunglasses. las gafas de sol, los lentes de sol. *lahs GAH-fahs deh sohl, lohs LEHN-tehs deh sohl.*

prescription. la prescripción. *lah preh-skreep-see-OHN.*

contact lenses. las lentillas. *lahs lehn-TEE-yahs.*
   soft. blandas. *BLAHN-dahs.*
   hard. de cristal. *deh kree-STAHL.*

cleaning solution. la solución limpiadora. *lah soh-loo-see-OHN leemp-eeAh-DOH-rah.*

saline solution. la solución salina. *lah soh-loo-see-OHN sah-LEE-nah.*

all-purpose solution.
la solución para limpiar y gruardar. *lah soh-loo-see-OHN PAH-rah leem-pee-AHR ee gwahr-DAHR.*

I lost a contact. He perdido una lentilla. *eh pehr-DEE-doh OO-nah lehn-TEE-yah.*

1135. Sanitary napkins, a sedative. Las toallas
higiénicas, un sedante. *lahs toh-AH-yahs ee-hee-
EH-nee-kahs, oon seh-DAHN-teh.*

1136. Shampoo. El champú. *ehl chahm-POO.*

1137. Shaving cream (lotion). La crema (loción) de afeitar.
lah KREH-mah (loh-see-OHN) deh ah-fay-TAHR.

1138. Soap, sunburn ointment. El jabón, el ungüento
para quemadura del sol. *ehl hah-BOHN, ehl oon-
GWEHN-toh PAH-rah keh-mah-DOO-rah dehl sohl.*

1139. Suntan lotion. El protector solar.
ehl proh-tehk-TOHR soh-LAHR.

1140. Tampon. El tampón. *ehl tahm-POHN.*

1141. A thermometer. Un termómetro.
oon tehr-MOH-meh-troh.

1142. Toothpaste. La pasta de dientes.
lah PAHS-tah deh dee-EHN-tehs.

Communications/*Comunicaciones*

Telephone/El teléfono

1143. Where may I telephone? ¿Dónde puedo telefonear?
DOHN-deh PWEH-doh teh-leh-foh-NEH-ahr?

1144. Will you make the call for me?
¿Quiere telefonear de mi parte?
kee-EH-reh teh-leh-foh-neh-AHR deh mee PAHR-teh?

1145. I want to make a local call to _____. Deseo
hacer una llamada local a _____. *deh-SEH-oh ah-
SEHR OO-nah yah-MAH-dah loh-KAHL ah _____.*

Quick & to the Point

Telephone. El teléfono. *ehl teh-LEH-foh-noh.*

Cell phone. El móvil. *ehl MOH-beel.*

What is your phone number? ¿Cuál es su número de teléfono?
kwahl ehs soo NOO-meh-roh deh teh-LEH-foh-no?

The line is busy. La línea está ocupada.
lah LEE-neh-ah ehs-TAH oh-koo-PAH-dah.

Can I use your phone? ¿Podría usar su teléfono?
poh-DREE-ah OO-sahr soo teh-LEH-foh-noh?

I will call you tomorrow. Yo le llamo mañana.
yoh leh YAH-moh mah-NYAH-nah.

May I speak to _____? ¿Puedo hablar con _____?
PWEH-doh AH-blahr kohn _____?

1146. **A long-distance call.**
Una llamada de larga distancia. *OO-nah yah-MAH-dah deh LAHR-gah dees-TAHN-see-ah.*

1147. **The operator will call you.** La telefonista le llamará.
lah teh-leh foh-NEES-tah leh yah-mah-RAH.

1148. **I want number _____.** Quiero el número _____.
kee-EH-roh ehl NOO-meh-roh _____.

1149. **Hello.** Aló or bueno or dígame.
ah-LOH or BWEH-noh or DEE-gah-meh.

1150. **Bye.** Adiós. *ah-dee-OHS.*

1151. **They do not answer.** No contestan.
noh kohn-TEHS-tahn.

Hello—Goodbye on the telephone.

How you say hello, when you answer the phone, varies from one country to another. You can answer:

Hellos

¡Hola! Used almost anywhere.

¡Sí! Also widely accepted.

¡Diga! Used in Spain.

¡Aló! Used in the Americas.

¡Oigo! Caribbean

¡Bueno! Mexico

Goodbyes

¡Adiós! The usual word for goodbye.

¡Chau! Widely used informal goodbye.

¡Hasta luego! Informal, see you later.

Me toca irme, chau. I have to go, bye.

Spanish speakers often end with:

Saludos a su familia. Greetings to your family.

1152. **The line is busy.** La línea está ocupada.
lah LEE-neh-ah ehs-TAH oh-koo-PAH-dah.

1153. **Dial it again.** Llame otra vez.
YAH-meh OH-trah behs.

1154. **May I speak to _____.** Deseo hablar con _____.
deh-SEH-oh AH-blahr kohn _____.

1155. He (she) is not in. Él (ella) no está.
ehl (EH-yah) noh ehs-TAH.

1156. This is _____ speaking. Habla _____.
AH-blah _____.

1157. Please take a message for _____.
Por favor tome un mensaje para _____. *pohr fah-BOHR TOH-meh oon mehn-SAH-heh PAH-rah _____.*

1158. My number is _____.
Mi número de teléfono es_____.
mee NOO-meh-roh deh-teh-LEH-foh-noh ehs _____.

1159. My cell phone number is _____.
Mi número de móvil (celular) es _____. *mee NOO-meh-roh deh MOH-beel (se-loo-LAHR) ehs _____.*

1160. Give me "a jingle." Échame un grito.
EH-chah-meh oon GREE-toh.

1161. Cell phone charger. Cargador de teléfono celular.
kahr-gah-DOHR deh the-LEH-foh-noh she-loo-LAHR.

1162. Can I have your telephone number?
¿Me da su número de teléfono?
meh dah soo NOO-meh-roh deh teh-LEH-foh-noh?

1163. Please call me. Llámeme, por favor.
YAH-meh-meh pohr fah-BOHR.

1164. May I use your phone? ¿Puedo usar su teléfono?
PWEH-doh oo-SAHR soo teh-LEH-foh-noh?

1165. What's the area (dialing) code for _____?
¿Cuál es el prefijo de _____?
kwal ehs ehl preh-FEE-hoh deh _____?

1166. **I'd like a phone card, please.**

Quiero una tarjeta para llamar por teléfono, por favor.   *kee-EH-roh OO-nah tahr-HEH-tah PAH-rah yah-MAHR pohr teh-LEH-foh-noh, pohr fah-BOHR.*

1167. **Where's the nearest phone booth?**

¿Dónde está la cabina más cercana?   *DOHN-deh ehs-TAH lah ka-BEE-nah mahs sehr-KAN-nah?*

1168. **What´s the number for information (directory assistance)?**

¿Cuál es el número de información?   *kwal ehs ehl NOO-meh-roh deh een-fohr-mah-see-OHN?*

1169. **I'd like to reverse the charges (call collect).**

Quiero llamar por cobro revertido.   *kee-EH-roh yah-MAHR pohr KOH-broh reh-behr-TEE-doh.*

1170. **Speak louder (more slowly) please.**

Hable más alto (despacio), por favor.   *AH-bleh mahs AHL-toh (dehs-PAH-see-oh), pohr-fah-BOHR.*

1171. **Hold on, please.**   Espere, por favor.
eh-PEH-reh, pohr-fah-BOHR.

1172. **I have to go now.**   Tengo que irme.
TEHN-goh keh EER-meh.

1173. **Nice to speak to you.**

Me encantó hablar con usted.
meh ehn-kahn-TOH ah-BLAHR kohn oos-TEHD.

1174. **I'll be in touch.**   Nos mantendremos en contacto.
nohs mahn-tehn-DREH-mohs ehn kohn-TAHK-toh.

Cell Phones/ Teléfonos Celulares, (Teléfonos Móviles)

1175. Where can I buy a cell phone?

Dónde puedo comprar un teléfono celular (móvil)?

DOHN-deh PWEH-doh kohm-PRAHR oon teh-LEH-foh-noh seh-loo-LAHR (MOH-beel)?

1176. I would like to buy a chip.

Me gustaría comprar una ficha.

meh goos-tah-REE-ah kohm-PRAHR OO-nah FEE-chah.

1177. Can I buy more time? ¿Puedo comprar más minutos?

PWEH-doh kohm-PRAHR mahs mee-NOO-tohs?

1178. How do you receive calls?

¿Cómo se reciben llamadas?

KOH-moh seh reh-SEE-behn yah-MAH-dahs?

1179. How do I make calls? ¿Cómo se hacen llamadas?

KOH-moh seh AH-sehn yah-MAH-das?

1180. Will this work in other countries?

¿Funcionará esto en otros países?

foon-see-oh-nah-RAH EHS-toh ehn oh-trohs pah-EE-sehs?

Quick & to the Point

Cell phone. El teléfono celular, el teléfono móvil.

ehl teh-LEH-foh-noh seh-loo-LAHR, ehl teh-LEH-foh-noh MOH-beel.

Where is a cell phone shop?

¿Dónde hay una tienda de teléfonos móviles? *DOHN-deh I OON-ah tee-EHN-dah deh teh-LEH-fohn-ohs MOH-beel-ehs?*

Check with your phone company to see if your phone can be used in the country you are visiting. You may find it more economical to buy an inexpensive cell phone when you arrive at your destination. You may need a new SIM card as you move into other countries. A more expensive option is a tri-band phone, which also works in North America.

1181. Where is the charger?   ¿Dónde está el cargador?
DOHN-deh-ehs-TAH ehl kahr-gah-DOHR?

1182. Text message, video message.   El mensaje de texto, el mensaje de vídeo.   *ehl mehn-SAH-heh deh TEHKS-toh, ehl mehn-SAH-heh deh BEE-dee-oh.*

1183. Send.   Enviar.   *ehn-bee-AHR.*

Social Networking/*Redes Sociales*

Both Facebook and Twitter offer the option to change the language preferences easily, so when when using them in other countries, you can continue to use the English version if you like.

Facebook

1184. News.   Las noticias.   *lahs noh-TEE-see-ahs.*

1185. Most recent (headlines).   Los titulares más recientes.   *lohs tee-too-LAH-rehs mahs reh-see-EHN-tehs.*

147

1186. Home. El inicio. *ehl ee-NEE-see-oh.*

1187. Profile. El perfil. *ehl pehr-FEEL.*

1188. Application requests. Las solicitudes de aplicaciones. *lahs soh-lee-see-TOO-dehs deh ah-plee-kah-see-OH-nehs.*

1189. Friends, messages, events. Los amigos, los mensajes, los eventos. *lohs ah-MEE-gohs, lohs mehn-SAH-hehs, lohs eh-BEHN-tohs.*

1190. Language. El idioma. *ehl ee-dee-OH-mah.*

1191. Chat friends. Los amigos de chat. *lohs ah-MEE-gohs deh chaht.*

Spanish Terms of Endearment/ Palabras de Cariño en Español

kiss besar	**love** el amor
hug abrazar	**hugs and kisses** besos y abrazos
love at first sight el flechazo	**to be in love** estar enamorado

Words for your boyfriend or girlfriend

la novia girlfriend	**el novio** boyfriend
mi amor my love	**mi corazón** my heart
cariño/a honey	**mi vida** my life
tesoro/a treasure	**nene/nena** baby
muñeca doll	**querido/a** loved one

1192. Friend search. Buscar amigos.
boos-KAHR ah-MEE-gohs.

1193. Account. La cuenta. *lah KWEHN-tah.*

Twitter

1194. What's happening? ¿Qué pasa? *keh PAH-sah?*

1195. Who's following? ¿A quién seguir?
ah KEE-ehn seh-GEER?

1196. Home. El inicio. *ehl ee-NEE-see-oh.*

1197. Direct messages. Los mensajes directos.
lohs mehn-SAH-hehs dee-REHK-tohs.

1198. Favorites. Los favoritos. *lohs fah-boh-REE-tohs.*

1199. Retweets. Los retweets. *lohs reh-TWEETS.*

1200. Current themes. Los temas del momento.
lohs TEH-mahs dehl moh-MEHN-toh.

1201. Change. Cambiar. *kahm-bee-AHR.*

1202. Following. Siguiendo. *see-gee-EHN-doh.*

1203. Home profile. El inicio perfil.
ehl ee-NEE-see-oh pehr-FEEL.

1204. Search for people. Buscar gente.
boos-KAHR HEN-teh.

1205. Help. Ayuda. *ah-YOO-dah.*

1206. Close session. Cerrar sesión.
seh-RRAHR seh-see-OHN.

1207. Second postings. Seguidores. *seh-gee-DOH-rehs.*

Useful Information/*Información Util*

Days of the Week/*Días de la Semana*

1208. Monday, Tuesday. Lunes, martes.
LOO-nehs, MAHR-tehs.

1209. Wednesday, Thursday. Miércoles, jueves.
mee-EHR-coh-lehs, HWEH-behs.

1210. Friday, Saturday. Viernes, sábado.
bee-EHR-nehs, SAH-bah-doh.

1211. Sunday. Domingo. *doh-MEEN-goh.*

Months, Seasons, Weather/*Meses, Estaciones, Clima*

1212. January, February. Enero, febrero.
eh-NEH-roh, feh-BREH-roh.

1213. March, April. Marzo, abril. *MAHR-soh, ah-BREEL.*

1214. May, June. Mayo, junio. *MAH-yoh, HOO-nee-oh.*

1215. July, August. Julio, agosto.
HOO-lee-oh, ah-GOHS-toh.

1216. September, October. Septiembre, octubre.
sehp-tee-EHM-breh. ohk-TOO-breh.

1217. November, December. Noviembre, diciembre.
noh-bee-EHM breh, dee-see-EHM-breh.

1218. Spring, summer. La primavera, el verano.
lah pree-mah-BEH-rah, ehl beh-RAH-noh.

1219. Autumn, winter. El otoño, el invierno.
ehl oh-TOH-nyoh, ehl een-bee-EHR-noh.

1220. It is warm (cold).   Hace calor (frío).
AH-seh kah-LOHR (FREE-oh).

1221. It is sunny (bad weather).   Hace sol (mal tiempo).
AH-seh sohl (mahl tee-EHM-poh).

1222. It is raining.   Llueve.   *yoo-EH-beh.*

1223. It is snowing.   Nieva.   *nee-EH-bah.*

1224. Foggy, cloudy.   Nebuloso, nublado.
neh-boo-LOH-soh, noo-BLAH-doh.

1225. The sun, sunny, shady.   El sol, soleado, con sombra.
el sohl, soh-leh-AH-do, cohn SOHM-brah.

Time and Time Expressions/La Hora y Términos del Tiempo

1226. What time is it?   ¿Qué hora es?   *keh OH-rah ehs?*

1227. It is one o'clock.   Es la una.   *ehs lah OO-nah.*

1228. It is five thirty.   Son las cinco y media.
sohn lahs SEEN-koh ee MEH-dee-ah.

1229. It is quarter after five.   Son las cinco y cuarto.
sohn lahs SEEN-koh ee KWAHR-toh.

1230. It is a quarter to six.   Son las seis menos cuarto.
sohn lahs sehs MEH-nohs KWAHR-toh.

1231. At 7:10 a.m.   A las siete y diez (de la mañana).
ah lahs see-EH-teh ee dee-EHS (deh lah mah-NYAH-nah).

1232. At ten to nine (p.m.).
A las nueve menos diez (de la noche).   *ah lahs noo-EH-beh MEH-nohs dee-EHS (deh lah NOH-cheh).*

1233. It is late.   Ya es tarde.   *yah ehs TAHR-deh.*

1234. In the afternoon.   Por la tarde.   *pohr lah TAHR-deh.*

1235. In the morning (evening).   Por la mañana (la noche).
pohr lah mah-NYAH-nah (lah NOH-cheh).

1236. Day, night, midnight, noon.
El día, la noche, la medianoche, el mediodía.
ehl DEE-ah, lah NOH-cheh, lah meh-DEE-ah-NOH-cheh, ehl meh-dee-oh-DEE-ah.

1237. Yesterday, last night.   Ayer, anoche.
ah-YEHR, ah-NOH-cheh.

1238. Today, tonight.   Hoy, esta noche.
oy, EHS-tah NOH-cheh.

1239. Tomorrow.   Mañana.   *mahn-YAH-nah.*

1240. (The) day before yesterday.   Anteayer.   *Ah-teh-ah-YEHR.*

1241. Last year (month).   El año (el mes) pasado.
ehl AH-nyoh (ehl mehs) pah-SAH-doh.

1242. Last Monday.   El lunes pasado.
ehl LOO-nehs pah-SAH-doh.

1243. Next week.   La semana próxima.
lah seh-MAH-nah PROHKS-ee-mah.

1244. Two weeks ago.   Hace dos semanas.
AH-seh dohs seh-MAH-nahs.

Numbers/*Los Números*

1245. One, two, three. Uno, dos, tres. *OO-noh, dohs, trehs.*

1246. Four, five, six. Cuatro, cinco, seis. *KWAH-troh, SEEN-koh, sehs.*

1247. Seven, eight, nine. Siete, ocho, nueve. *see-EH-teh, OH-choh, noo-EH-beh*

1248. Ten, eleven, twelve. Diez, once, doce. *dee-EHS, OHN-seh, DOH-seh.*

1249. Thirteen, fourteen. Trece, catorce. *TREH-seh, kah-TOHR-seh.*

1250. Fifteen, sixteen. Quince, dieciséis. *KEEN-seh, dee-ehs-ee-SEH-ees.*

1251. Seventeen, eighteen. Diecisiete, dieciocho. *dee-eh-see-see-EH-teh, dee-eh-see-OH-choh.*

1252. Nineteen, twenty. Diecinueve, veinte. *dee-eh-see-noo-EH-beh, BEYN-teh.*

1253. Twenty-one, twenty-two. Veintiuno, veintidós. *beyn-tee-OO-noh, beyn-tee-DOHS.*

1254. Thirty, thirty-one. Treinta, treinta y uno. *TREYN-tah, TREYN-ta ee OO-noh.*

1255. Forty, fifty. Cuarenta, cincuenta. *kwah-REHN-tah, seen-KWEN-ta.*

1256. Sixty, seventy. Sesenta, setenta. *seh-SEHN-tah, seh-TEHN-tah.*

1257. Eighty, ninety. Ochenta, noventa.
oh-CHEHN-tah, noh-BEHN-tah.

1258. One hundred, one hundred one. Cien, ciento uno.
SEE-ehn, see-EHN-toh OO-noh.

1259. Two hundred, three hundred.
Doscientos, trescientos.
doh-see-EHN-tohs, treh-see-EHN-tohs.

1260. Four hundred, five hundred.
Cuatrocientos, quinientos.
Kwah-troh-see-EHN-tos, kee-nee-EHN-tohs.

1261. Six hundred, seven hundred.
Seiscientos, setecientos.
seys-see-EHN-tohs, seh-teh-see-EHN-tohs.

1262. Eight hundred, nine hundred.
Ochocientos, novecientos.
oh-choh-see-EHN-tohs, noh-beh-see-EHN-tohs.

1263. One thousand, two thousand. Mil, dos mil.
meel, dohs meel.

1264. First, second. Primero, segundo.
pree-MEH-ro, seh- GOON-doh.

1265. Third, fourth. Tercero, cuarto.
tehr-SEH-roh, KWAHR-toh.

1266. Fifth, sixth. Quinto, sexto. *KEEN-toh, SEHKS-toh.*

1267. Seventh, eighth. Séptimo, octavo.
SEHP-tee-moh, ohk-TAH-boh.

1268. Ninth, tenth. Noveno, décimo.
noh-BEH-noh, DEH-see-moh.

Measurement/*Medidas*

1269. What is the length (width)?
¿Qué largo (ancho) tiene?
keh LAHR-goh (AHN-choh) tee-EH-neh

1270. How much per meter? ¿Cuánto por metro?
KWAHN-toh pohr MEH-troh?

1271. What size is it? ¿De qué tamaño es?
deh keh tah-MAH-nyoh ehs?

1272. It is ten meters long by four meters wide.
Tiene diez metros de largo por cuatro metros de
ancho.
*tee-EH-neh dee-EHS MEH-trohs deh LAHR-goh pohr
KWAH-troh MEH-trohs deh AHN-choh.*

1273. Large, small, medium. Grande, pequeño, mediano.
GRAHN-deh, peh-KEH-nyo, meh-dee-AH-noh.

1274. High, low. Alto, bajo. *AHL-toh, BAH-hoh.*

1275. Alike, different. Igual, diferente.
ee-GWAHL, dee-feh-REHN-teh.

1276. A pair, a dozen. Un par, una docena.
oon pahr, OO-nah doh-SEH-nah.

1277. A handful. Un puñado. *oon poo-NYAH-doh.*

1278. 50%. Cincuenta por ciento.
seen-KWEHN-tah pohr see-EHN-toh.

1279. Half a dozen. Media docena.
MEH-dee-ah doh-SEH-nah.

1280. Half a meter. Medio metro. *MEH-dee-oh MEH-troh.*

USEFUL INFORMATION

Colors/Colores

1281. Light, dark. Claro, oscuro. *KLAH-roh, ohs-KOO-roh.*

1282. Black, blue, brown. Negro, azul, café or marrón.
NEH-groh, ah-SOOL, kah-FEH, or *mah-RROHN.*

1283. Cream, gray, green. Crema, gris, verde.
KREH-mah, grees, BEHR-deh.

1284. Orange, pink, purple. Anaranjado, rosado, morado.
ah-nah-rahn-HAH-doh, rro-SAH-doh, moh-RAH-doh.

1285. Red, white. Rojo, blanco. *RROH-hoh, BLAHN-koh.*

1286. Yellow. Amarillo. *ah-mah-REE-yoh.*

1287. I want a lighter (darker) shade.
Quiero un tono más claro (más oscuro). *kee-EH-roh
oon TOH-noh mahs KLAH-roh (mahs ohs-KOO-roh).*

Common Objects/Objetos Ordinarios

1288. Ashtray. El cenicero. *ehl seh-nee-SEH-roh.*

1289. Bag. La bolsa. *lah BOHL-sah.*

1290. Bobby pins. Las horquillas. *lahs ohr-KEE-yahs.*

1291. Box. La caja. *lah KAH-hah.*

1292. Bulb (light). La bombilla. *lah bohm-BEE-yah.*

1293. Candy. Los dulces. *lohs DOOL-sehs.*

1294. Can opener. El abrelatas. *ehl ah-breh-LAH-tahs.*

1295. Cloth (cotton, silk, wool, linen).
La tela (de algodón, de seda, de lana, de lino).
*lah TEH-lah (deh ahl-goh-DOHN, deh seh-dah, deh
lah-nah, de lee-noh).*

1296. Computer (laptop). La computadora portátil. *lah kohm-poo-tah-DOH-rah por-TAH-teel.*

1297. Corkscrew. El sacacorchos. *ehl sah-kah-COHR-chohs.*

1298. Cushion. El cojín. *ehl coh-HEEN.*

1299. Doll. La muñeca. *lah moo-NYEH-kah.*

1300. Earring. El arete. *ehl ah-REH-teh.*

1301. Flashlight. La linterna eléctrica. *lah leen-TEHR-nah eh-LEHK-tree-kah.*

1302. Glasses (sun). Los lentes (de sol). *lohs LEHN-tehs deh sohl.*

1303. Gold. El oro. *ehl OH-roh.*

1304. Gum. El chicle. *ehl CHEE-kleh.*

1305. Hairpin. La horquilla. *lah ohr-KEE-yah.*

1306. Hook. El ganchito. *ehl gahn-CHEE-toh.*

1307. Iron. La plancha. *lah PLAHN-chah.*

1308. Jewelry. Las joyas. *lahs HOY-yahs.*

1309. Leather. El cuero. *ehl KWEHR-oh.*

1310. Linen. El lino. *ehl LEE-noh.*

1311. Mosquito net. El mosquitero. *ehl mohs-kee-TEHR-roh.*

1312. Nail file. La lima de uñas. *lah LEE-mah deh OO-nyahs.*

1313. Necklace. El collar. *ehl koh-YAHR.*

1314. Needle. La aguja. *lah ah-GOO-hah.*

1315. Notebook. El cuaderno. *ehl kwah-DEHR-noh.*

1316. Padlock. El candado. *ehl kahn-DAH-doh.*

1317. Pail. El cubo. *ehl KOO-boh.*

1318. Penknife. El cortaplumas. *ehl kohr-tah-PLOO-mahs.*

1319. Perfume. El perfume. *ehl pehr-FOO-meh.*

1320. Pin (ornamental). El broche. *ehl BROH-cheh.*

1321. Pin (straight). El alfiler. *ehl ahl-fee-LEHR.*

1322. Radio. El radio. *ehl RRAH-dee-oh.*

1323. Rayon. Rayón. *rrah-YOHN.*

1324. Ring. El anillo. *ehl ah-NEE-yoh.*

1325. Rubbers. Los zapatos de caucho.
lohs sah-PAH-tohs deh KAHW-choh.

1326. Safety pin. El imperdible. *ehl eem-pehr-DEE-bleh.*

1327. Scissors. Las tijeras. *lahs tee-HEH-rahs.*

1328. Shoe lace. El cordón de zapatos.
ehl cohr-DOHN deh sah-PAH-tohs.

1329. Silk. Seda. *SEH-dah.*

1330. Silver. Plata. *PLAH-tah.*

1331. Stone (precious). La piedra (preciosa).
lah pee-EH-drah (preh-see-OH-sah).

1332. Stopper. El tapón. *ehl tah-POHN.*

1333. Strap. La correa. *lah koh-RREH-ah.*

1334. Straw. La paja. *lah PAH-hah.*

1335. Thimble. El dedal. *ehl deh-DAHL.*

1336. Thread. El hilo. *ehl EE-loh.*

1337. Toy. El jugete. *ehl hoo-GEH-teh.*

1338. Umbrella.   El paraguas.   *ehl pah-RAH-gwahs.*

1339. Vase.   El florero.   *ehl flo-REH-rroh.*

1340. Video games.   Los videojuegos.   *lohs bee-dee-oh-HWEH-gohs.*

1341. Washcloth.   Una toallita para lavarse la cara.   *OO-nah toh-ah-YEE-tah PAH-rah lah-BAHR-seh lah KAH-rah.*

Metric Conversion Tables

LENGTH

1 centímetro (cm.) = 2/5 pulg.
1 metro (m.) = 100 cms. = 39 pulg.
1 kilómetro (km.) = 1,000 m. = 5/8 milla.
1 pulgada (pulg.) = 2½ cms.
1 pie = 30 cms.
1 yarda (yd.) = 90 cms.

WEIGHT

1 gramo = .036 oz.
1000 gramos = 3½ oz.
1 kilo = 1,000 gramos = 2 lbs. 2 oz.
1 onza (oz.)= 28 gramos.
1 libra (lb.) = 453 gramos.

CAPACITY

1 pinta = .47 litro.
1 cuarto = .95 litro.
1 galón = 3.76 litros.

1342. Watch.   El reloj.   *ehl rreh-LOH*

1343. Wire.   El alambre.   *ehl ah-LAHM-breh.*

1344. Wood.   La madera.   *lah mah-DEHR-ah.*

1345. Wool.   De lana.   *deh LAH-nah.*

1346. Zipper.   La cremallera, el cierre.
lah kreh-mah-YEH-rah, ehl see-EH-rreh.

NATIVE FOOD AND DRINK LIST

This food supplement consists mainly of native Spanish dishes. We have however also included a selection of Latin American, South American, and Mexican dishes, all of which show strong Spanish influences. All foods have been alphabetized in Spanish to make menu reading easier. Typical and standard American foods can be found in the restaurant section of the text.

Note that dining hours in Spain, Latin and South America are distinctly later than they are in the United States. Breakfast is simple, usually rolls and coffee served between 8–11 a.m. Lunch is leisurely and substantial, and is served between 1–3 p.m. and usually followed by a siesta. Dinner or supper is customarily served after 9 p.m., but more likely after 10 p.m. The custom of stopping at 5 p.m. for cocktails or coffee and a snack is very characteristic of Spanish life. It is typical of Spanish night life to begin extremely late and to continue far into the night.

Sopas/Soups
Aperitivos/Appetizers
Tapas/Tapas

Aceitunas (rellenos). (Stuffed olives).

Albóndigas. Meatballs.

Almejas. Clams.

Calamares. Squid.

Calderada. Fish soup; a variety of bouillabaisse.

161

NATIVE FOOD AND DRINK LIST

Caldo. Chicken broth.

Caldo de pimento. Pepper soup.

Callos. Tripe in hot paprika sauce.

Caracoles. Snails.

Chorizo. Spicy sausage.

Entremeses. Appetizers.

Espárragos. Asparagus.

Fondos de alcachofas. Hearts of artichokes with oil and vinegar.

Gazpacho. Chilled vegetable soup made with cucumbers, tomatoes, red pepper, onions, garlic, bread crumbs, oil, and vinegar.

Jamón. Ham.

Mejillones. Mussels.

Pimientos. Peppers.

Pinchos. Grilled skewered meat.

Potaje de garbanzos. Thick pea soup made with chick peas.

Potaje de habas secas. Thick bean soup made with dried beans.

Patatas bravas. Thick fried potato slices served with a spicy sauce.

Queso manchego. Hard yellow cheese from La Mancha.

Salmorejo. Chilled soup similar to Gazpacho.

Sancocho de camarones. Shrimp chowder.

Sopa castellana. Baked garlic soup with chunks of ham and a poached egg.

Sopa de agrino. Potato and watercress soup.

Sopa de ajo. Garlic soup usually served with a poached egg.

Sopa de ajo blanco con uvas. Garlic soup with grapes.

Sopa de albóndigas. Soup with meatballs made with a tomato base and served with small fried meatballs in it.

Sopa de almendras. Purée of almond soup.

Sopa de camarones. Shrimp soup.

Sopa de cebolla. Onion soup.

Sopa de cocido. A kind of broth, with beef, ham, sausage, chick peas, cabbage, turnip, onion, garlic and potatoes.

Sopa de coles. Cabbage soup.

Sopa de cuarto de hora. Fish soup made of fish and shell-fish and served with hard boiled eggs, peas and toasted bread.

Sopa de galápagos. Turtle soup.

Sopa de legumbres. Vegetable soup.

Sopa de mariscos. Seafood soup.

Sopa de ostras. Oyster soup.

Sopa de pan con gambas. Bread soup with prawns.

Sopa de pescado. Fish soup prepared with one kind of fish or a variety of native fish.

NATIVE FOOD AND DRINK LIST

Sopa de puchero. Thick beef soup.

Sopa de rana. Frog soup.

Sopa de tomate. Tomato soup.

Sopa de verduras. Vegetable soup.

Sopa española. Soup made with rice, tomatoes, peppers, and spices.

Tapas. Small snacks taken with a drink before meals consisting of olives, almonds, cheese, fish, and anchovies.

Tortilla. Round Spanish omelet served in many varieties either hot or cold.

Pescado/Fish
Mariscos/Shellfish

Abadejo. Cod.

Ali-pebre dángulles. Eel in garlic, oil, and paprika sauce.

Almejas. Clams.

Almejas con arroz. Clams and rice.

Anguilas. Eels.

Arenques. Herring.

Atún. Tuna.

Atún en escabeche. Pickled tuna.

Bacalao. Dried cod fish.

Besugo. Sea bream.

Bogavante. Lobster.

Bonito. Bonito.

Boquerones. Fish very much like anchovies.

Caballa. Mackerel.

Calamares. Squid.

Calamares en su tinta. Squid simmered in its own ink.

Caldereta asturiana. Mixed fish stew.

Callos, mondongo. Tripe.

Camarones. Shrimp.

Cangrejos. Crabs.

Caracoles. Snails.

Chanquetes. Small thin fried fish.

Chocos con habas. Cuttlefish/large squid with broad beans.

Chupe. Thick fish stew.

Cígalas. Sea crayfish.

Coquines. Cockles.

Escabeche. Pickled fish.

Gambas. Large shrimp.

Huachinango. Red snapper.

Lamprea. Lamprey.

Langosta. A variety of lobster.

Lenguado. Sole.

Lisa. Grey mullet.

Llobarro. Bass.

NATIVE FOOD AND DRINK LIST

Lubina. Sea bass.

Mariscos. Shellfish.

Marmita. Fish stew in which bonito is predominant.

Mejillones. Mussels.

Merluza. Codfish.

Mero. Grouper/perch/sea bass.

Mítulos rellenos. Stuffed mussels.

Ostras. Oysters.

Paella. Popular Spanish dish prepared with chicken, shell-fish, sausage, pimiento, and saffron flavored rice.

Paella de mariscos. Paella with seafood.

Paella valenciana. Paella with chicken, shrimp, mussels, prawns, squid, peas, tomato, chili pepper, garlic.

Pargo encebollado. Red bream baked with onions.

Pescado blanco en ajillo. White fish with garlic.

Pescado con arroz. Fish with rice.

Pescado con salsa de coco. Fish with a coconut sauce.

Pez espada en amarillo. Swordfish cooked with herbs.

Pulpo. Octopus.

Raya en pimentón. Skate and red pepper.

Róbalo. Trout/haddock.

Rodaballo. Flounder/turbot.

Rollo de pescado. Fish roll.

Sábalo. Shad.

Salmón. Salmon.

Sardinas. Sardines.

Trucha. Trout.

Zarzuela. Mixture of seafoods prepared in a spice sauce.

Carne/Meat
Aves/Poultry
Especialidades/Specialties

Ajiaco. Meat, chicken, pepper, avocado, and potatoes prepared in a stew.

Ajoqueso. Latin American dish of melted cheese and peppers.

Albondigón. Meatloaf.

Arroz con pollo. Chicken with rice.

Arroz a la parellada. Rice prepared with chicken, meat, and vegetables.

Biftec or **bistec.** Steak.

Berenjena rellena. Stuffed eggplant.

Butifarra. Pork sausage.

Cabeza de ternera. Calf's head with with vinaigrette sauce.

Cabrito asado. Roast leg of spring lamb.

Caldo gallego. Thick stew of meat and vegetables.

NATIVE FOOD AND DRINK LIST

Cazuela de cordero. Lamb stew made with corn, peas, beans, rice, potatoes, and herbs.

Cebollas y frijoles. Bean stuffed onion.

Chanfaina. Goat entrails with vegetables.

Cholupas. Spicy Mexican dish prepared with sausage and vegetables.

Chorizo. Garlic and pork sausage.

Chuletas de cerdo. Pork cutlets.

Chuletas de cordero. Lamb cutlets.

Chuletas de ternera. Veal cutlets.

Cocido. Boiled meat with ham, bacon, sausage, and vegetables.

Cochinillo asado. Roast suckling pig.

Codornices asadas. Roast quail.

Cola de vaca. Oxtail.

Conejo. Rabbit.

Cordero en ajillo pastor. Lamb stew.

Corona de cordero. Crown of lamb.

Costillas de cerdo. Spareribs.

Costillas de cordero a la parrilla. Grilled lamb chops.

Croqueta de pollo. Chicken croquettes.

Croquetas de papas con carne. Meat and potato cakes.

Empanadas. Meat pies.

Empanadillas. Small pastries filled with meat.

NATIVE FOOD AND DRINK LIST

Enchiladas. Mexican corn tortilla stuffed with meat, cheese, and chile.

Estofado. Stew made with diced chicken, beef, lamb, ham, onions, tomatoes, herbs, and wine.

Fabada asturiana. Pork and beans.

Frijolada. Bean stew with bacon and ham.

Frijoles. Beans with bacon and ham.

Fritos de lentejas. Fried lentils.

Fritura mixta. Assorted meat, chicken or fish and vegetables, fried in deep fat.

Gallina. Chicken.

Gallina con garbanzos. Stewed chicken with chick peas.

Guisado español. Stew made with beef, onions and olive oil.

Higado de ternera a la parrilla. Grilled calf's liver.

Humita. Pancake made with fresh corn, tomato, pimento, sugar, and oil.

Ignames con ron. Sweet potatoes prepared with rum and sherry.

Jamón. Ham of the region.

Jamón aguadilla. Roast fresh ham.

Jamón serrano. Smoked ham.

Jigote. Meat hash.

Locro. Corn stew made with wheat, meat, and spices; popular in South America.

NATIVE FOOD AND DRINK LIST

Lomo a la parilla. Grilled pork chops.

Longaniza. Pork sausage.

Medallones con champiñones. Filet of beef or veal with mushrooms.

Menudo gitana. Well seasoned tripe.

Mole de guajalote. Mexican dish made with turkey in a sauce of garlic, onions, tomatoes, tortillas, and chocolate.

Mole poblano. Chicken with sauce of chili pepper, chocolate, and spices.

Mondongo. Seasoned tripe stew.

Morcilla. Blood sausage.

Morcilla blanca. Sausage made with chicken, bacon, hard-boiled eggs, and spices.

Olla podrida. Stew made with ham and chick peas.

Paella. Native Spanish dish prepared with chicken, seafood, sausage, onions, garlic, tomatoes, pimento, and saffron flavored rice. There are many varieties of paella.

Pato con cereza. Braised duck with cherry sauce.

Pavo asado. Roast turkey.

Pecho de ternera. Breast of veal.

Pelota. Chopped beef.

Pepitoria de gallina. Chicken stew made with olives, tomatoes, and vegetables.

Perdices asadas. Roast partridge.

Perdíz. Partridge.

Picadillo. Hash.

Pichones. Squabs, pigeons.

Pie de cerdo bretona. Pigs knuckles with beans.

Pierna de cordero. Leg of lamb.

Pimientos rellenos. Stuffed peppers.

Pisto manchego. Stew made with onions, eggs, and pork.

Pollo asado frío con ensalada. Chicken salad.

Pollo con naranja. Chicken prepared with an orange sauce.

Pote gallego. Stew prepared with beef, ham, sausage, and vegetables.

Puchero. Boiled dinner made of meat and vegetables.

Puerco estofado. Spicy, pork stew.

Redondo asado. Roast veal.

Riñones. Kidneys.

Riñones al jerez. Kidneys prepared in a sherry sauce.

Rollo de Santiago. Meatloaf covered with potatoes.

Ropa vieja. Meat hash.

Rosbif. Roast beef.

Salchichas. Veal and pork sausage.

Salchichón. Pork and bacon sausage.

Salpicón de ave. Chicken with mayonnaise.

Sancocho. Stew of meat, yucca, and bananas.

Sesos. Brains.

NATIVE FOOD AND DRINK LIST

Simplón frito. Fried noodles.

Solomillo. Filet of veal.

Suculento. Vegetable dish prepared with corn squash and other native vegetables.

Tallarines. Noodles.

Tamale. A mixture of ground corn filled with minced chicken or meat and steamed.

Ternera asada fría. Cold roast veal.

Torta de conejo. Rabbit tart.

Tortas de carne. Meat patties.

Tortilla, Mexican. A thin, flat unleavened corn cake.

Tortilla, Spanish. An omelet.

Tortilla con jamón. Ham omelet.

Tortilla española. Spanish omelet.

Tortilla de sardinas. Sardine omelet.

Tostón asado. Roast suckling pig.

Tasajo. Corned beef.

Ensaladas/Salads

Ensalada de pepino. Cucumber salad.

Ensalada de tomate. Tomato salad.

Ensalada variada. Mixed green salad.

Postres/Desserts

Alfajores. Small round cookies filled with dulce de leche.

Almendrado. Macaroon.

Arroz con leche. Rice with milk.

Bizcocho. Sponge cake.

Brazo de gitano. Rum cream roll.

Budín. Pudding.

Buñuelos. Donuts.

Cabello de ángel. Jam made from a gourd, called sidra.

Canutillos. Custard horns with cinnamon.

Capirotada. Sweet pudding made with bread and cinnamon.

Carne de membrillo. Preserved quince.

Churros. Light pastry dough rolled into long thin strips, fried, and rolled in sugar.

Compota. Stewed fruit.

Crema catalana. Caramel pudding (crème brulée).

Crema española. Dessert made of eggs, milk, and gelatin.

Flan. Caramel custard: a classic Spanish dessert.

Flan cremoso. Boiled custard.

Galletas. Cookies.

Gelatina. Gelatin.

Guayaba. Guava.

NATIVE FOOD AND DRINK LIST

Helados. Ice creams.

Higo en almíbar. Figs in syrup.

Magdalenas. Cupcakes.

Mantecado. Rich almond ice cream.

Mantecadas de almendras. Almond biscuits.

Mazapán. Marzipan.

Membrillo. Jellied dessert made of quince.

Melón. Melon.

Merengue. Meringue.

Migas. Fried bread.

Mostachones. A kind of gingerbread.

Natilla. Custard.

Pastas. Pastries.

Pastel de queso. Cheesecake.

Pasteles. Cakes.

Pastelitos. Small cakes.

Perruñas. Little biscuits.

Piña. Pineapple.

Pudín. Pudding.

Roscas. Cookies.

Rosquillas. Biscuits shaped in the form of rings.

Sandía. Watermelon.

Sorbete. Sherbet.

Suspiros. Little fried cakes sprinkled with sugar.

Tarta. Tart, pie.

Tarta de manzana. Apple tart.

Tarteletas. Small tarts.

Torta. Cake.

Torta de almendras. Almond tart.

Tortera. Pastry.

Turrón. Nougat dessert.

Yemas. Candy dessert made with egg yolks, sugar, fruits, nuts; formed into small balls.

Quesos/Cheeses

Burgos. A soft, creamy cheese named after the province that originated it.

Cabrales. Somewhat like blue cheese.

Manchego. Hard Spanish cheese made with ewe's milk.

Perilla. A firm, bland cheese made from cow's milk, sometimes known as *teta*.

Queso de bola. Cheese made from cow's milk and eaten fresh, similar to Dutch edam.

Queso de cabra. Goat's milk cheese.

Queso gallego. Medium soft cheese.

Requesón. Soft, white cheese similar to cottage cheese.

NATIVE FOOD AND DRINK LIST

Bebidas/Drinks

Anís. Anise.

Aperitivio. Aperitif.

Cerveza. Beer.

Champaña. Champagne.

Chicha. Fermented maize or pineapple drink.

Coñac. Brandy.

Gaseosa. Soda.

Ginebra. Gin.

Guarapo. Potent alcoholic drink made from sugar cane.

Jerez. Sherry.

Oporto. Port.

Ponche. Punch.

Pulque. Strong, fermented drink.

Refresco. Soda (soft drink)

Sangría. Chilled red wine, fruit juice, brandy, soda, and often pieces of fruit.

Sidra. Alcoholic cider.

Vino. Wine.

Vino blanco. White wine.

Vino de Borgoña. Burgundy wine.

Vino corriente. Ordinary table wine.

Vino de Rosado. Rosé wine.

Vino de la tierra. Local wine.

Vino spumoso. Sparkling wine.

Vino tinto. Red wine.

Bebidas Sin Alcohol/Non-Alcoholic Drinks

Agua (helada, mineral). Water (iced, mineral).

Batida. Milkshake.

Café. Coffee.

Café con leche. Coffee with milk.

Café descafeinado. Decaffeinated coffee.

Chocolate caliente. Hot chocolate.

Leche. Milk.

Limonada. Lemonade.

Naranjada. Orangeade.

Refresco. Soda pop.

Soda. Soda water.

Té. Tea.

ENGLISH-SPANISH DICTIONARY

Some words in this dictionary have endings like this: *abogado/a*. Use the a ending when referring to a female. Nouns have gender in Spanish, so they will be listed with their definite articles. Feminine nouns will be preceded by *la* and masculine nouns will be preceded by *el*.

A

able (adj.) capaz

able (v.) poder

aboard a bordo

above encima

accelerator el acelerador

accent el acento

accept aceptar

accident el accidente

accommodation el alojamiento

across a través

activist el/la activista

actor el actor

actress la actriz

adapter el adaptador electrónico

addiction la dependencia, la adicción

address la dirección

address, e-mail la dirección de correo electrónico

adhesive tape la cinta adhesiva or el esparadrapo

admire admirar

adult el adulto

advantage la ventaja

advice el consejo

afraid miedoso/a

afraid (to be afraid of) tener miedo de

after después

afternoon la tarde

ENGLISH-SPANISH DICTIONARY

again otra vez

against contra

aggressive agresivo/a

agree estar de acuerdo

agriculture la agricultura

ahead delante

aid la ayuda

AIDS el SIDA

air el aire

air-conditioned aire acondicionado

airline la aerolínea

air mail el correo aéreo

airplane el avión

airport el aeropuerto

aisle el pasillo

alarm clock el despertador

alcohol el alcohol

algebra el álgebra

alike igual

all todo

allergic alérgico/a

allergy la alergia

all right vale, está bien

almond paste el marzapán

almost casi

alone solo/a

already ya

also también

altar el altar

altarpiece el tablero

although aunque

altitude la altura

always siempre

amateur el/la aficionado/a

ambassador el embajador/la embajadora

among entre

ambulance la ambulancia

amusements las diversiones

analgesic el analgésico

ancient antiguo/a

and y

anemia la anemia

anesthetic el anestésico

angry enfadado/a

ankle el tobillo

annual anual

another otro/a

answer (n.) la repuesta

answer (v.) contestar

answering machine el contestador automático

ant la hormiga

antenna la antena

antibiotic el antibiótico

antiques las antigüedades

antiseptic el antiséptico

any alguno/a

apartment el apartamento

appendicitis la apendicitis

appendix el apéndice

appetizers los aperitivos

apple la manzana

appointment la cita

apricot el damasco, el albaricoque

April abril

apron el delantal

arcades los portales

archaeology la arqueología

architecture la arquitectura

argue discutir

arm el brazo

aromatherapy la aromaterapia

arrivals llegadas

arrive llegar

art el arte

art gallery la galería de arte

arthritis la artritis

artist el/la artista

arts (native) la artesanía

artwork la obra de arte

as big as tan grande como

ashtray el cenicero

Asian asiático/a

ask (a question) preguntar

ask (for something) pedir

asparagus el espárrago

aspirin la aspirina

asthma el asma

astronaut el/la astonauta

astronomer el/la astrónoma/o

at a

at (@ sign) arroba

at least por lo menos

at that time para aquel entonces

at times a veces

athlete el/la atleta, el/la deportista

atmosphere la atmósfera

attend asistir

attic el ático

attend asistir

audioguide el audioguía

aunt la tía

automatic teller el cajero automático

automobile el automóvil, el auto

autumn el otoño

avenue la avenida

away fuera

awful horrible, fatal

B

baby el/la bebé, niño/a

baby carseat el asiento para el coche

baby food la comida para bebé

baby formula la fórmula de bebé

babysitter el niñero/la niñera

back (adj.) atrás

back (n.) la espalda

backpack la mochila

bacon el tocino

bad mal, malo/a

bag la bolsa

bag, plastic la bolsa de plástico

bag, ziplock la bolsa de cremallera

baggage el equipaje

baggage check facturación de equipajes

baggage claim reclamación de equipajes

baked horneado/a

bakery la panadería

balcony el balcón

ball la pelota

ballet el ballet

balloon el globo

ballpark figure la cifra aproximada

ballroom la sala de fiestas

banana el plátano, el guineo

band el grupo

bandage la venda

Bandaid la curita

bank el banco

baptism el bautizo

bar la barra, la cantina

bartender el barman, el/la cantinero/a

barber el/la peluquero/a

barber shop la barbería, la peluquería

bargain sale la ganga

baseball el béisbol

basement el sótano

basket el cesto, la canasta

basketball el baloncesto

bat el bate

bath el baño

bathrobe la bata de baño, el albornoz

bathroom el baño, el servicio

bathing cap el gorro de baño

bathing suit el traje de baño

bathtub la bañera

battery la pila, la batería

battery (car) la batería

be ser, estar

beach la playa

beak el pico

beans los frijoles

bear (n.; animal) el oso

bear (v.) aguantar

beard la barba

beautiful bonito/a

beauty salon la peluquería

because porque

become hacerse

bed la cama

bedroom el dormitorio, la alcoba, la habitación

bed sheet la sábana

beef la carne de vaca, la carne de res

beer la cerveza

bees las abejas

before antes de

begin comenzar, empezar

beggar el/la mendigo/a

begin comenzar

behavior comportamiento

behind detrás de

bell la campana

bellman el botones

belly la barriga

belong pertenecer

below abajo

belt el cinturón

berth (on a train) la litera

beside al lado de

besides además de

best el/la mejor

better mejor

between entre

bib el babero

Bible la Biblia

bicycle la bicicleta
big grande
bike la bici
bill la cuenta
billiards el billar español
binoculars los prismáticos
biodegradable biodegradable
biography la biografía
bird el pájaro
birth certificate la partida de nacimiento
birth control pills la píldora anticonceptiva
birthday el cumpleaños
birthday cake el pastel de cumpleaños
biscuit el bizcocho
bite (sting) la picadura
bite (dog) la mordedura
bite (v.) morder
black negro/a
blackberry la mora
bladder la vegija
blame someone else echar la culpa a otro/a
blanket la manta, la cobija
bleeding sangrado
bless bendecir

blender la licuadora
blind ciego/a
blister la ampolla
block la cuadra, la manzana
blond rubio/a
blood la sangre
blood group el grupo sanguíneo
blood pressure la tensión presión arterial
blouse la blusa
blue azul
blueberry el arándano
board embarcar, abordar
boarding pass la tarjeta de embarque
boat el barco
bobby pin la horquilla
body el cuerpo
boil (n.) un divieso, una pústula
boil (v.) hervir
bologna la mortadela
bolt el tornillo
bomb la bomba
bone el hueso
book el libro
book (make a reservation) reservar

bookstore la librería

booster seat (for children) el asiento alto (para niños)

boots las botas

border la frontera

boric acid el ácido bórico

boring aburrido/a

born nacido/a

borrow pedir prestado

boss el jefe

bother molestar

bottle la botella

bottle opener el abrebotellas

bottom el fondo

boulevard el bulevar

bowl el plato hondo

box la caja

boxing el boxeo

boy el chico, el muchacho

boyfriend el novio

bra el sostén, el sujetador

bracelet la pulsera

brake el freno

brains los sesos, el cerebro

branch la rama

branch office la sucursal

brandy el coñac, el aguardiente

brass el latón

brave bravo/a

bread el pan

break (a leg, an arm, etc.) quebrarse

break (in general) romper

break (rest) descansar

break (tear) romper

breakfast el desayuno

breast el pecho

breasts los senos

breath el aliento

breathe respirar

bribe el soborno

bridge el puente

brief breve

briefcase la maleta

brilliant sobresaliente

bring traer

broken roto

bronchitis el bronquitis

broom la escoba

broth el caldo

brother el hermano

brown marrón

browser el navegador

bruise una contusión

brush el cepillo
bucket el cubo
Buddhist el/la budista
bugs los bichos
build construir
building el edificio
bulb (light) la bombilla
bull el toro
bull fight la corrida de toros
bull ring la plaza de toros
bunk bed la litera
burn (n.) la quemadura
burn (v.) quemar
burp el eructo
bus el autobús
bus stop la parada de autobuses
business el negocio
business card la tarjeta de visita
business person el/la comerciante
busker el/la cantante callejero/a
busy ocupado/a
but pero
butter la mantequilla
butterfly la mariposa

buttocks las nalgas
button el botón
buy comprar
by en
by the way a propósito

C

cabbage la col, el repollo
cabin la cabina
cabin on a ship la camarote
cable car el teleférico
cable TV el cable
café el café
cake el pastel, la tarta
calculator la calculadora
calendar el calendario
calf el ternero
call llamar
calorie la caloría
camera la cámara
camp acampar
camper la caravana
camping el camping
can (n.) la lata
can (v.) poder
canal el canal
canary el canario
cancel cancelar
candle la vela

candy los dulces, las golosinas, el caramelo

candy store la dulcería

cane el bastón

canoe la canoa

can opener el abrelatas

canvas el lienzo

cape la capa

captain el capitán

car el carro, el automóvil, el coche

car, dining (train) el coche comedor

car registration la matrícula

car, sleeping (train) el coche cama

carafe la garrafa

card la tarjeta

card, playing el naipe

card, telephone la tarjeta telefónica

care (about something) preocuparse

care (for someone) cuidar de

careful cuidadoso/a

caring bondadoso/a

carousel el carrusel, el tiovivo

carpenter el/la carpintero/a

carpet la alfombra

carpet, wall-to-wall la alfombra moqueta

carrots las zanahorias

carry cargar, llevar

carry-on luggage el equipaje de mano

carseat (baby) el asiento para bebés

carton el cartón

cartoons los dibujos animados

cash el dinero en efectivo

cashier el cajero/a

cash machine el cajero automático

cash register la caja registradora

cast (plaster) el yeso

cast el reparto

castle el castillo

castle (Moorish) el alcázar

cat el gato

catalog el catálogo

catastrophe la catástrofe

cathedral la catedral

Catholic católico/a

catsup la salsa de tomate
cauliflower el coliflor
cave la cueva
celebrate celebrar
cell phone el teléfono móvil, el celular
cell phone store la tienda de teléfonos móviles
cellar la bodega
cemetery el cementerio
center el centro
centimeter el centímetro
century el siglo
ceramic la cerámica
cereal el cereal
certificate el certificado
chains las cadenas
chair la silla
chalk la tiza
champagne la cava, el champán
championship el campeonato
chance la oportunidad
change (n.) el cambio
change (v.) cambiar
changing room el vestuario
channel el canal

chapel la capilla
charge cargar
charger el cargador
charming encantador/a
chat room el chat room
cheap barato/a
cheaper más barato
cheat (n.) el/la tramposo/a
check (money) el cheque
check (restaurant) la cuenta
check (tires) (v.) revisar
check-in (desk) la facturación de equipajes
checkmate jaque mate
checkroom el vestuario, el guardarropa
cheek la mejilla
cheers (a toast) salud
cheese el queso
chemistry la química
cherry la cereza
chess el ajedrez
chessboard el tablero de ajedrez
chest el baúl
chest (on the body) el pecho
chest pains dolor del pecho

chew masticar
chewing gum el chicle
chicken el pollo
chick peas los garbanzos
child el/la niño/a
chilis los chiles
chills los escalofríos
chin la barbilla
Chinese chino/a
chlorine el cloro
chocolate el chocolate
chocolate, hot el chocolate caliente
choir el coro
command el mandato
chop (n.) la chuleta
choose escoger
Christian el cristiano/la cristiana
Christmas La Navidad
Christmas Eve La Nochebuena
church la iglesia
church service el servico
cigarettes los cigarillos
cigars los cigarros
cigar store la cigarrería
cinema el cine
circle el círculo
circus el circo

city la ciudad
city center el centro de la ciudad
city walls las murallas
class la clase
class, first la primera clase
class, second la segunda clase
classical clásico/a
classical art el arte clásico
clean (adj.) limpio/a
clean (v.) limpiar
cleaning fluid el quitamanchas
clear claro/a
client el/la cliente/a
cliff el acantilado
climb subir
clinic la clínica
cloak el capote, la capa
cloakroom el guardarropa
clock el reloj
clock, alarm el despertador
close (v.) cerrar
close (near) cerca de
closed cerrado
closet el amario

cloth la tela

clothing la ropa

clothing store la tienda de ropa

cloud la nube

cloudy nublado

clown el payaso

coach el entrenador/la entrenadora

coast la costa

coat el abrigo

coat hanger la percha

cockroach la cucaracha

cocktail el cóctel

coffee el café

coffee shop la cafetería

coin la moneda

cold (adj.) frío/a

cold (n.) el resfriado, el catarro

cold cream la crema para la cara

cold cuts los fiambres, los embutidos

cold water el agua fría

collar el cuello

collarbone la clavícula

colleague el/la colega

collect (telephone) el cobro revertido

college la universidad

colors los colores

comb el peine

come venir

comedy la comedia

comet el cometa

comfortable cómodo/a

communication la comunicación

communion la comunión

compact disc, CD el disco compacto, el CD

companion el/la compañero/a

company la compañía

compass la brújula

complain quejarse

complicated complicado/a

computer la computadora, el ordenador

computer games los juegos de ordenador

conceited presumido/a

concert el concierto

condiments los condimentos

conditioner el acondicionador

conductor el conductor

confession la confesión

confident seguro/a

confirm confirmar

conflict el conflicto

congestion la congestión

congratulations felicidades

connection enlance

conservative conservador, conservadora

considerate considerado/a

constipation el estreñimiento

construction la construcción

consulate el consulado

contact lenses las lentillas

contagious contagioso/a

contraceptives los anticonceptivos

contract el contrato

convenience food la comida de preparación rápida

convent el convento

cook (person) el/la cocinero/a

cook (v.) cocinar

cool fresco

cool (slang) guay

copper el cobre

copy la copia

cordless phone el teléfono inalámbrico

cork el corcho

corkscrew el sacacorchos

corn el maíz, el elote

corn pads los parches para los callos

corner (exterior) la esquina

corner (interior) el rincón

corrupt corrupto/a

corridor el pasillo

cost (n.) el costo, el precio

cost (v.) costar

cot el catre, la cama portátil

cotton el algodón

cotton candy el algodón de azúcar

cough la tos

cough (v.) toser

cough drops las gotas para la tos

count contar

country code el código

country (nation) país

country(side) el campo

coupon el cupón

court (legal) el juzgado, el tribunal

court (tennis) la cancha, la pista

cousin el/la primo/a

cover (v.) tapar

cover (cap) la tapa

cover charge el precio de admisión

cow la vaca

cozy cómodo/a

crab el cangrejo

crafts las artesanías

crafty habilidoso/a, ingenioso/a

cramp el calambre

crane (bird) la grulla

crazy loco/a

cream (dairy) la nata

cream (color) crema

cream, first-aid la crema de primeros auxilios

credit card la tarjeta de crédito

creep (slang) el/la desgraciado/a

crew la tripulación

crime el crimen

criticize criticar

cross (n.) la cruz

crossroads la encrucijada

crossword puzzle el crucigrama

crowd (n.) la multitud, el muchedumbre

crutches las muletas

cry (v.) llorar

cucumber el pepino

cuddle (n.) el abrazo

cup la taza

cupboard el armario

curator el conservador/la conservadora

curtain la cortina

curve la curva

cushion el cojín

custard la natilla, el flan

custom (habit) la costumbre

customs la aduana

cut cortar

cycle (v.) montar en bicicleta

cycling el ciclismo

cystitis la cistitis

D

dad el papá

daily diariamente

dairy products los productos lácteos
dance (n.) el baile
dance (v.) bailar
danger el peligro
dangerous peligroso/a
dark oscuro/a
dark, to get anochecer
dash (-) guión
date (appointment) la cita
date (on calendar) la fecha
daughter la hija
dawn la madrugada
day el día
day after tomorrow pasado mañana
day before yesterday anteayer
day, the other el otro día
dead muerto/a
deaf sordo/a
death la muerte
December diciembre
decide decidir
deck la cubierta
deck of cards una baraja
declare declarar

decongestant descongestionante
deep profundo/a
deer el ciervo
degree el título
delay el retraso
delete borrar
delicatessen la charcutería, la fiambrería
delay la demora, el retraso
delayed retrasado/a
delicious delicioso/a
deliver repartir
demanding exigente
democracy la democracia
demonstration la manifestación
dental floss la seda dental, el hilo dental
dentist el/la dentista
denture la dentadura
deny negar
deodorant el desodorante
depart salir de, partir
department store el almacén
departures las salidas

ENGLISH-SPANISH DICTIONARY

depilatory el depilatorio

deposit el depósito

descendant el descendiente

desert el desierto

deserve merecer

desire las ganas

design el diseño

dessert el postre

destination el destino

destroy destruir

detail el detalle

develop desarrollar, revelar

diabetes la diabetes

diabetic diabético/a

diamond el diamante

diaper el pañal

diaper rash el escozor de pañal

dial marcar

diarrhea la diarrea

diary la agenda

dice los dados

dictionary el diccionario

die morir

diet la alimentación

different diferente

difficult difícil

difficulties las dificultades

dine cenar

dining car (train) el coche comedor

dining room el comedor

dinner la cena

direct directo/a

director el director/la directora

direction la direccíon

dirt la suciedad

dirty sucio/a

disabled minusválido/a

disadvantage la desventaja

disappear desaparecer

discount el descuento

discover descubrir

discrimination la discriminación

disease la enfermedad

dishes los platos

disinfectant el desinfectante

dismissal el despido

display (electronic screen) la pantalla

distributor la distribuidora

disturb molestar

diving el buceo
divorced divorciado/a
dizziness el vértigo
do hacer
dock el muelle
doctor el doctor, la doctora
documentary el documental
dog el perro
doll la muñeca
dome la cúpula
dominion (computer) el dominio
donkey el burro
door la puerta
dormitory el dormitorio
dot (.com, etc.) el punto
double (adj.) doble
double (v.) doblar
double bed la cama de matrimonio
double room la habitación doble
doughnut el buñelo
doubt dudar
download bajar
down (stairs) abajo
downtown el centro
dozen la docena

draft beer la cerveza de barril
drama el drama
dramatic dramático/a
draw dibujar
dream (n.) el sueño
dream (v.) soñar
dress (n.) el vestido
dress (v.) ponerse, vestirse
dress (a wound) curar a
drink (n.) el bebido
drink (v.) beber, tomar
drive conducir, manejar
driver (person) el chofer
driver (electronic) la unidad
driver's license el carnet de conducir, el permiso de conducir
drug la medicina
drums la batería
drop dejar caer
drops las gotas
drugstore la farmacia
drunk borracho/a
dry (adj.) seco/a
dry (v.) secar
dry cleaner la tintorería
dryer la secadora

dubbed doblado/a

duck el pato

dungeon el calabozo

dusk anochecer

duty-free libre de impuestos

dysentery la disentería

E

each cada

eagle el águila

ear la oreja

earache dolor de oído

early temprano

earn ganar

earplug el tapón de oídos

earring el arete, el pendiente

earth la tierra

earthquake el terremoto

east el este

Easter la Pascua

easy fácil

eat comer

economy la economía

editor el editor, la editora

education la educación

eggs los huevos

elbow el codo

election la elección

elevator el acensor

electrical adaptor el adaptador electrónico

electricity la electricidad

elevator el ascensor

e-book el libro electrónico

e-commerce el comercio electrónico

e-mail el correo electrónico

e-mail address la dirección de correo electrónico

e-ticket el billete electrónico, el pasaje electrónico

embarrassing embarazoso/a

embassy la embajada

emerald la esmeralda

emergency la emergencia

emergency exit la salida de emergencia

emergency room la sala de urgencias

employee el/la empleado/a

employer el jefe/la jefa

empty vacío/a

end (v.) terminar

endangered species las especies en peligro de extinción

engagement el compromiso

engine el motor

engineer el/la ingeniero/a

England Inglaterra

English el inglés

enjoy disfrutar, gozar

enlargement la amplicación

enough bastante, suficiente

enter entrar

entertaining entretenido/a, divertido/a

entrance la entrada

envelope el sobre

environment el medio ambiente

epilepsy la epilepsia

epsom salts la sal de heno

equal opportunity la igualdad de oportunidades

equality la igualdad

eraser el borrador

etching el aguafuerte

Europe Europa

European el/la europeo/a

evening la noche

evening dress el vestido largo

event el acontecimiento

every todo/a

every day cada día

every month cada mes

every year cada año

everything todo/a

exactly exactamente

exaggerate exagerar

example el ejemplo

excellent excelente

except excepto

excess exceso/a

exchange (n.) el cambio

exchange (v.) cambiar

exchange rate el tipo de cambio

exciting emocionante

excursion la excursión

excuse (n.) la excusa

excuse (v.) disculpar, excusar

exhausted agotado/a

exhibit exponer

exit la salida

expensive caro/a

explain explicar

exploration la exploración

express expreso

express mail el correo urgente

eye el ojo

eyebrow la ceja

eyelash la pestaña

eyelid el párpado

eye liner el lápiz de ojos

eye shadow la sombra de ojos

F

fabric la tela

face la cara

facial el facial

factory la fábrica

fail fracasar

faint desmayarse

fair (just) justo/a

fall caer

fall (autumn) el otoño

false falso/a

family la familia

famous famoso/a

fan (handheld) el abanico

fan (electric) el ventilador

fan (of a team) el fanático, el hincha

fantastic fantástico/a

far lejos

fare el pasaje, la tarifa

farm la granja

farmer el/la granjero/a

fashion la moda

faster más rápido

fat (adj.) gordo/a

fat (n.) la grasa

father el padre

father-in-law el suegro

faucet el grifo

fault la culpa

fax el fax

fear (v.) temer

February febrero

feel sentirse

feelings los sentimientos

fence la cerca

fencing la esgrima

female femenino/a

ferry el transbordador
festival el festival
fever la fiebre
few poco/a
fiction la ficción
field el campo
fight (n.) la pelea
fight (v.) discutir
figures las cifras
fill llenar
film el cine, la película
fine (good) bien
finger el dedo
fingernail la uña
finish (v.) terminar,
    acabar
fir el abeto
fire el fuego
fire (uncontrolled) el
    incendio
fireplace la chimenea
fireworks los fuegos
    artificiales
first primero/a
first aid los primeros
    auxilios
first-aid cream la crema
    de primeros auxilios
fish (n.) el pez, el
    pescado (when on the
    menu)

fish (v.) pescar
fit caber
fix arreglar, fijar
fizzy gaseoso/a
flag la bandera
flash (on camera) el
    flash
flash drive la memoria
    instantánea
flashlight la linterna
flavor el sabor
flea la pulga
flea market el rastro
flight el vuelo
flight attendant el/la
    auxiliar de vuelo
flip-flops las chancletas
flock of birds la
    bandada de aves
floor el suelo
floor (in a building) el
    piso
floss, dental la seda
    dental
flour la harina
flower la flor
flower market la
    floristería
flu el gripe
fly (n.) la mosca
fly (v.) volar

ENGLISH-SPANISH DICTIONARY

fog la niebla
follow seguir
food la comida
food poisoning la intoxicación alimentaria
foot el pie
football (soccer) el fútbol
football (American) el fútbol americano
footpath el sendero
for por, para
for now por ahora
forbidden prohibido/a
foreign extranjero/a
forest el bosque
forget olvidar
forgive perdonar
fork el tenedor
formula (baby) la leche para bebés
foundation (makeup) la base para la cara
fontain la fuente
forecast el pronóstico
foreign language la lengua extranjera
forgive perdonar
fox el zorro
foyer el vestíbulo
fracture la fractura

fragile frágil
France Francia
free (no cost) gratis
free libre
freeze congelar
French el francés
French fries las papas fritas
Friday el viernes
fried frito/a
friend el/la amigo/a
friendly sociable, amistoso/a
friendship la amistad
frisbee el frisbee
from de
from time to time de vez en cuando
front (in — of) en frente de, delante de
frosty helado
frown el ceño
frozen congelado/a
frozen foods los productos congelados
fruit la fruta
fruit (stewed) la compota
full lleno/a
fun la diversión
funeral el funeral

funny divertido/a, gracioso/a, chistoso/a
furniture el mueble
furnished amueblado/a
fuses los fusibles
future el futuro

G

gallery la galería
game el juego, el partido (sporting event)
game show el concurso
garage el garaje
garage (mechanic) el taller
garbage la basura
garden el jardín
garden, vegetable la huerta
garlic clove el diente de ajo
gas la gasolina
gas station la gasolinera
gate la puerta
gauze la gasa
general general
generous generoso/a
gentleman el caballero
genuine auténtico/a
geometry la geometría

German el alemán
get lost hasta nunca
get off bajarse
get up levantarse
gifts los regalos
gig la actuación
girl la chica
girlfriend la novia
give dar
glacier el glaciar
glad (to be glad) alegrarse
glad feliz
glass (container) el vaso
glass (clear material) el vidrio
glasses los lentes, las gafas
gloves los guantes
go ir
go away irse
go back volver
go through atravesar
goal el gol, la meta
goat la cabra
God Dios
going ir a
gold el oro
golf el golf
good bueno/a

ENGLISH-SPANISH DICTIONARY

good day buenos días
goodbye adiós
good health buena salud
gorilla el gorila
gossip (v.) chismear
gossipy chismoso/a
Gothic el gótico
Gothic-Islamic el/la mudéjar
government el gobierno
grade la nota
gram el gramo
granddaughter la nieta
grandfather el abuelo
grandmother la abuela
grandson el nieto
grapefruit la toronja
grapes las uvas
grass la hierba
grave (n.) la tumba
gray gris
greasy grasiento/a
great fantástico/a
Great Britain Gran Bretaña
great-grandfather el bisabuelo
great-grandmother la bisabuela
green el verde

greetings los saludos
grocery store la tienda de comestibles, el supermercado
guarantee la garantía
guava la guayaba
guess (v.) adivinar
guest el/la invitado/a
guide el guía
guidebook la guía
guide dog el perro lazarillo
guided tour la gira con guía
guinea pig el conejillo de indias
guilty culpable
guitar la guitarra
gum el chicle
gums las encías
gun la pistola
gymastics la gimnasia
gynecologist el/la ginecólogo/a

H

hair el pelo
hair dye el tinte de pelo
hairbrush el cepillo de pelo
haircut el corte de pelo

hairdresser el/la peluquero/a

hairpin la horquilla

half medio/a

half-brother/sister medio/a hermano/a

hall (corridor) el pasillo

hall (room) la sala

hallucinate alucinar

ham el jamón

hammer el martillo

hammock la hamaca

hand la mano

hand in entregar

hand lotion la crema de manos

handicapped el/la minusválido/a

handicrafts las artesanías

handle el tirador

handlebars el manillar

handkerchief el pañuelo

handmade hecho a mano

handsome guapo/a

hang up colgar

hangers las perchas

happiness la felicidad

happy feliz, contento/a

happy birthday feliz cumpleaños

harbor el puerto

hard duro/a

hard (difficult) difícil

hardware store la ferretería

hare la liebre

harrassment el acoso

hash el jogote, el picadillo

hat el sombrero

hat shop la sombrerería

hate (v.) odiar

have tener

hay fever la fiebre de heno

he él

head la cabeza

head waiter el/la jefe/a de camareros, el/la jefe/a de meseros

headache el dolor de cabeza

headlights los faros

headphones los auriculares

health la salud

health insurance el seguro de efermedad

healthy saludable

hear oír

hearing aid el audífono

heart el corazón

heat el calor

heater el radiador

heaven el cielo

heavy pesado/a

heel el talón

hello hola

helmet el casco

help! (exclamation) ¡socorro!

help (n.) la ayuda

help (v.) ayudar

helpful útil

hen la gallina

herbalist el/la herborista

herbs las hierbas

here aquí

hi hola

hiccup el hipo

high alto/a

high chair la silla para niños, la trona

high school el colegio

higher más alto/a

hike ir de excursión

hiking boots las botas de montaña

hill la colina

hip la cadera

history la historia

hitchhike hacer autostop

hoarseness la ronquera

hobby el pasatiempo

hockey el hockey

hole el agujero

holiday el festivo

Holy Week La Semana Santa

homeless (n.) los sin hogar

homemade hecho en casa

homesick la nostálgico

honest honesto/a

honey la miel

honeymoon la luna de miel

hook el gancho

hope (v.) esperar

horns los cuernos

horrible horrible

hors d'oeuvres los aperitivos

horse el caballo

horse riding montar a caballo

hospital el hospital

host el anfitrión

hostess la anfitriona
hot (warm) caliente
hot (spicy) picante
hot chocolate el chocolate caliente
hotel el hotel
hot water bottle la bolsa para agua caliente
hour la hora
house la casa
how cómo (when it's a question), como
how long cuánto, cuánto tiempo
how much cuánto
hug el abrazo
human rights los derechos humanos
hungry tener hambre
hurry de prisa
hurricane el huracán
hurt (v.) doler
husband el esposo, el marido
hyphen (-) el guión

I

I yo
ice el hielo

ice bag la bolsa para hielo
ice cream el helado
ice cubes los cubos de hielo
ice water el agua helada
idle vago/a
identification la identificación
if si
ill enfermo/a
illness la enfermedad
immediately inmediatamente
immigration la inmigración
important importante
imported importado/a
Impressionist (adj.) impresionista
in en
in general por lo general
in that time en aquella época
include incluir
included incluido
incredible increíble
independent independiente
indigestion la indigestión
industry la industria

ENGLISH-SPANISH DICTIONARY

inexpensive barato/a
infection la infección
inflammation la inflamación
influenza el gripe
information la información
injection la inyección
injured herido/a
ink la tinta
inner tube la cámara
innocent inocente
insect el insecto
insect repellent el repelente de insectos
inside dentro de, interior
instant instante
instead en vez de
instructor el profesor, la profesora
insurance el seguro
insured asegurado/a
intense intenso/a
intelligent inteligente
interest interés
interesting interesante
intermission el intermedio
Internet el Internet

Internet access el acceso a Internet
Internet café el café de Internet
international internacional
intersection la encrucijada
interview la entrevista
intestines los intestinos
introduce presentar
invitation la invitación
iodine el yodo
Ireland Irlanda
iron (metal) el hierro
iron (appliance) la plancha
ironing board la mesa de planchar
is es
island la isla
Italian el italiano
Italy Italia
itch (n.) la picazón
itch (v.) picar
itinerary el intinerario

J

jack el gato
jacket la chaqueta

jail la cárcel
jam la mermelada
January enero
jar la jarra
jaw la mandíbula
jealous celoso/a
jeans los vaqueros
jeep el jeep, el todo terreno
jelly la jalea
jewelry las joyas
jewelry store la joyería
Jewish judío/a
job el trabajo, el oficio
joint la coyuntura
joke el chiste
journalist el/la periodista
journey el viaje
juice el jugo, el zumo
judge el/la juez
July julio
jump saltar
junction el cruce
junk food la comida chatarra, la comida basura
June junio
just as I am tal como soy
justice la justicia

K

keep guardar
keep out prohibir la entrada
ketchup la salsa de tomate
kettle la olla
key (for a lock) la llave
key (on electronics) la tecla
keyboard el teclado
kick (n.) la patada
kick (v.) empatar
kickoff el saque inicial
kidney el riñón
kill matar
kilogram el kilogramo
kilometer el kilómetro
kind amable
kindergarten el jardín infantil
king el rey
kitchen la cocina
kite la cometa
kitten el/la gatito/a
knee la rodilla
knife el cuchillo
knights los caballeros
knocked down atropellado/a

207

know (a person) conocer
know (a fact) saber

L

lace (trim) el encaje
lace (shoe) el cordón
ladies' room las damas, las señoras
lake el lago
lamb el cordero
land (n.) la tierra
land (v.) aterrizar
language el idoma, la lengua
laptop el ordenador portátil
large grande
larger más grande
last último/a
last month el mes pasado
last night anoche
last week la semana pasada
last year el año pasado
late tarde
later más tarde
latest el más tarde
laugh reír
laundry la lavandería

laundry soap el detergente
lavender la lavanda
law la ley
lawn el césped
lawn mower la cortadora de césped
lawyer el/la abogado/a
laxative el laxante
lazy perezoso/a
lead el plomo
leader el jefe, la jefa
league la liga
learn aprender
leather el cuero
leave salir
ledge el saliente
left (direction) la izquierda
(to be) left over (v.) quedar
leg la pierna
lemon el limón
lend prestar
length el largo
lens, contact las lentillas
Lent la Cuaresma
lentils las lentejas
less menos
letter la carta
lettuce la lechuga

liar el/la mentiroso/a
library la biblioteca
lice los piojos
lie (v.) mentir
lies (n.) las mentiras
life la vida
lifeboat la lancha
life preserver el salvavidas
light (adj.) ligero/a
light (n.) la luz
lighter (adj.) más claro, más ligero
lighter (n.) el encendedor
lights las luces
lights (clear) claro/a
like como
like (v.) gustar
line la línea
line (that you stand in) la fila
linen el lino
lip el labio
lip salve el cacao de labios
lipstick el lápiz de labios
liqueur el licor
list la lista
listen escuchar
liter el litro

little (small) pequeño
little (amount) poquito
live (adj.) vivo/a
live (v.) vivir
liver el hígado
living room la sala
lobster la langosta
local call la llamada local
lock (n.) la cerradura
lock (v.) cerrar
lockers los casilleros
lodging el alojamiento
lollipop el chupete
long largo/a
long distance larga distancia
look mirar
look after cuidar
look for buscar
look here mire
look out cuidado
lose perder
lose patience perder la paciencia
lost perdido/a
lot (a) mucho
lotion la loción
loud ruídoso/a
love (n.) el amor

love (v.) amar
lover el/la amante
low bajo/a
lower (v.) bajar
loyal leal
luck suerte
luggage el equipaje
luggage, carry-on el equipaje de mano
lukewarm tibio/a
lump el bulto
lunch el almuerzo
lung el pulmón
luxury el lujo

M

machine la máquina
mad enojado/a
made of hecho de
magazines las revistas
magician el/la mago/a
maid la criada, la camarera
mail el correo
mailbox el búzon
main principal
main dish el plato principal
make hacer

make a mistake cometer un error
makeup el maquillaje
male el varón
man el hombre
manager el gerente
manicure la manicura
many muchos/muchas
map el mapa
marble el mármol
March marzo
mare la yegua
market el mercado
market, flea el rastro
market, open air el mercado municipal
marmalade la mermelada
marriage el matrimonio
married casado/a
marry casarse
mascara el rímel
Mass la misa
massage el masaje
mass media los medios de comunicación masivos
mat la esterilla
match (game) el partido
matches los fósforos
matter el asunto

matter, doesn't no importa

mattress el colchón

maximum el/la máximo/a

May mayo

maybe quizás

mayor el/la alcalde

meal la comida

measurements las medidas

meat la carne

meat, chopped el salpicón

meat pie la empanada

mechanic el mecánico

medal la medalla

medicine la medicina

medicine dropper el gotero

medicine, non-aspirin substitute el Nolotil

medieval medieval

meditation la meditación

medium mediano/a

meet encontrar

melon el melón

member el/la miembro

men los hombres

mended remendado/a

men's room los señores, los hombres

menstrual cramps el dolor de la menstruación

menstruation la menstruación

menthol cigarettes los cigarrillos mentolados

menu el menú

merry-go-round el carrusel, el tiovivo

message el mensaje

message, text el SMS, el mensaje de texto

metal el metal

meter el metro

meteor el meteorito

Methodist el/la metodista

middle el medio

midnight la medianoche

migraine la migraña

military el ejército

milk la leche

million el millón

mind la mente

mineral water el agua mineral

minimum el mínima/la mínima

minute el minuto

mirror el espejo

Miss la señorita
miss (to be lacking) faltar
missing perdido/a
mistake el error
misunderstanding el malentendido
mix la mezcla
moat el foso
mobile phone el móvil
modem el módem
modern moderno/a
moisturizer el hidratante
moleskin la tela de piel de topo
mom la mamá
momento el momento
monastery el monasterio
Monday el lunes
money el dinero
money order el giro postal
monk el monje
monkey el mono
month, last el mes pasado
months los meses
monument el monumento
moon la luna
Moors los moros
more más

morning la mañana
mosque la mezquita
mosquito el mosquito
mosquito net el mosquitero
mother la mamá
mother-in-law la suegra
motivated motivado/a
mouse (computer) el ratón
mouth la boca
mouthwash el enjuage bucal
motorboat la motora
motor scooter la motocicleta
motorcycle el moto
mountain la montaña
mountain range la cordillera
mountaineering el alpinismo
mouse el ratón
moustache el bigote
mouth la boca
move (v.) mover
movies el cine
MP3 player el reproductor de MP3
Mr. Señor
Mrs. Señora

much mucho

mud el lodo

muggy húmedo

muscle el músculo

museum el museo

mushrooms los hongos, las setas, los champiñones

music la música

musician el/la músico/a

Muslim el musulman, la musulmana

mustard la mostaza

mute el/la mudo/a

mutton el carnero

my mi

N

nail (finger, toe) la uña

nail clipper la cortauñas

nail file la lima de uñas

nail polish el esmalte de uñas

nail polish remover el quitaesmaltes

naked desnudo/a

name el nombre

napkin la servilleta

narrow estrecho/a

national park el parque nacional

nationality la nacionalidad

nature la naturaleza

naturopath el/la naturópata

nausea la náusea

near cerca de

necessary necesario/a

neck el cuello

necklace el collar

neck tie la corbata

need (v.) necesitar

needle la aguja

neighbor el/la veciono/a

neighborhood el barrio

neither tampoco

nephew el sobrino

nerve el nervio

nervous nervioso/a

net la red

Netherlands Holanda

never nunca

new nuevo/a

news las noticias

newspaper el periódico

news stand el quiosco

New Year's Day el día de Año Nuevo

ENGLISH-SPANISH DICTIONARY

New Year's Eve la Nochevieja
New Zealand Nueva Zelanda
next próximo/a
next week la semana que viene
nice amable, simpático/a
nickname el apodo
niece la sobrina
night la noche
night, last anoche
night before last anteanoche
nightgown el camisón
no no
no vacancy lleno, completo
noise el ruido
noisy ruidoso/a
non-aspirin substitute substituto sin aspirina
non-fiction no ficción
non-smoking no fumadores
none nada
noodles los fideos
noon el mediodía
normal normal
north el norte

nose la nariz
nosy entrometido/a
not no
not yet todavía no
notebook el cuaderno
nothing nada
notify avisar
nougat el turrón
novel la novela
November noviembre
now ahora
nuclear nuclear
number el número
nun la monja
nurse el/la enfermero/a
nut la nuez
nylon (fabric) el nilón
nylons (pantyhose) las medias

O

oak el roble
obey obedecer
obvious obvio/a
occupation el oficio
occupied ocupado/a
ocean el océano
October octubre
of de
offense la ofensa

offer (v.) ofrecer

office la oficina

office supply store la papelería

often a menudo

oil (cooking) el aceite

oil (motor) el petróleo

O.K. O.K., vale

old viejo/a

olive la aceituna

olive oil el aceite de olivas

Olympic games los juegos olímpicos

omelet la tortilla

on en, sobre

on sale en oferta

on time puntual

once una vez

one-way ticket el billete sencillo

onion la cebolla

only sólo

open (adj.) abierto/a

open (v.) abrir

opening la inauguración

opera la ópera

operation la operación

operator (telephone) el/la telefonista

opinion la opinión

optician el/la óptico/a

or o

oral oral

orange (color) anaranjado/a

orange (fruit) la naranja

orangeade la naranjada

orchestra la orquesta

orchid la orquídea

order (n.) el orden

order (v.) pedir

ordinary corriente, normal

oregano el orégano

organ el órgano

organize organizar

organized organizado/a

original original

others los otros/las otras

out of order descompuesto/a

outside afuera

over (done) terminado/a

overcoat el abrigo

owe deber

owl el búho

own poseer

ENGLISH-SPANISH DICTIONARY

owner el/la dueño/a
ox el buey
oxygen el oxígeno
oysters las ostras
ozone layer la capa de ozono

P

pacifier el chupete
pack (v.) empacar, hacer la maleta
package el paquete
padlock el candado
page la página
pail el cubo
pain el dolor
pain in the neck el/la plasta, el dolor en el cuello
painkiller el analgésico
paint pintar
painter el pintor/la pintora
painting la pintura
paintings los cuadros
pair (couple) la pareja
pair (of gloves) par (de guantes)
pajamas el pijama
palace el palacio

palace (Moorish) el alcázar
pan la cazuela
panties las bragas
pants los pantalones
panty liner el salva slip
paper (wrapping) el papel de envolver
paper (writing) el papel
paper clip el gancho para papel
paraplegic el/la parapléjico/a
parcel post el paquete postal
parents los padres
park (n.) el parque
park (v.) aparcar, estacionar
parking lot el estacionamiento
parliament el parlamento
parrot el loro
parsley el perejil
part la parte
part (hair) la raya, la partidura
partridge la perdiz
party la fiesta
pass (n.) el pase

passenger el/la pasajero/a

passive pasivo/a

passport el pasaporte

past pasado/a

pastry el pastel

pastry shop la pastelería

path el sendero

patient (person) el/la paciente

patient paciente

patio el patio

pavement la acera

paws las patas

pay pagar

pay attention prestar atención

payment el pago

pay attention to hacer caso

peace la paz

peach el durazno, el melocotón

peak la cumbre

peanuts los cacahuates, los maníes

pear la pera

peas los guisantes, los chícharos

pedestrian el peatón, la peatona

pen el bolígrafo, la lapicera

pencil el lápiz

penicillin la penicilina

penknife el cortaplumas, la navaja

people la gente

pepper la pimienta

peppers los pimientos

pepper shaker el pimentero

percent por ciento

perch la percha

perfect perfecto/a

performance la representación, la actuación

perfume el perfume

perhaps quizás, tal vez

period (of time) el período

period (women's) la regla

permanent (wave) la permanente

permanent fijo/a, permanente

permit permitir

peroxide el agua oxigenada

person la persona

personal personal
personality la personalidad
perspire sudar
pet la mascota
petition la petición
pewter el peltre
pharmacy la farmacia
pheasant el faisán
phone el teléfono
phone booth la cabina telefónica
phone, mobile el teléfono móvil
photo la foto
photocopy la fotocopia
photography la fotografía
physics la física
pick escoger
pickles los encurtidos
pickpocket el/la carterista
picnic el picnic
pie la tarta
piece la pieza, el pedazo
pig el cerdo
pill la pastilla, la píldora
pillow la almohada

pillowcase la funda
pilot el/la piloto
pin el broche
pin (straight) el alfiler
PIN la clave secreta
pine el pino
pineapple la piña
pink rosado/a, rosa
pipe la pipa
pity la lástima
pizza la pizza
place (n.) el lugar
place (v.) poner
plain sencillo
plane el avión
planet el planeta
plant (n.) la planta
plant (v.) sembrar
plastic el plástico
plastic bag la bolsa de plástico
plate el plato
plateau la meseta
platform el andén, la plataforma
play (v.) jugar
play (theatre) la obra de teatro
play (music) tocar
play cards jugar a cartas

playground el área de jugar

playing cards los naipes

playpen el parque para niños

please por favor

pleasing agradable

pleasure el placer

pliers las pinzas

plug (bath) el tapón

plug (electrical) el enchufe

pneumonia la pulmonía

pocket el bolsillo

poetry la poesía

point (n.) el punto

point (v.) indicar, mostrar

poison el veneno

poisoning la intoxicación

poker el póquer

police el policía, la policía

police station la estación de policía

polite cortés

polka dots los lunares

pollen el polen

pollution la contaminación

polyester el poliéster

pool la piscina

pool (game) el billar americano

poor pobre

popcorn las palomitas de maíz

porcelain la porcelana

pork el puerco

port el puerto

porter el porteador, el maletero

portrait sketcher el/la caricaturista

Portugal Portugal

possible posible

postcard la tarjeta postal

postage el franqueo

poster el cartel

post office la oficina de correo

pot la olla

potato la papa, la patata

pottery la alfarería, la cerámica

poverty la pobreza

powder el polvo, el talco

power el poder

powerful poderoso/a

practical práctico/a

prayer la oración

prayerbook el devocionario

prefer preferir

pregnancy el embarazo

premiere el estreno

prepare preparar

Presbyterians los presbiterianos

prescription la receta

present (gift) el regalo

presentation la presentación

president el presidente/la presidenta

press (v.) planchar

press (news) la prensa

press conference la rueda de prensa

pressure la presión

pretty bonito/a, lindo/a

prevent prevenir

price el precio

pride el orgullo

priest el sacerdote

prime minister el primer ministro/la primera ministra

prince el príncipe

princess la princesa

print (art) el grabado

print (v.) imprimir

printed (fabric) estampado/a

printer la impresora

prison la cárcel, la prisión

prisoner el/la prisionero/a

private privado/a, particular

private tutor el/la profesor/a particular

problem el problema

producer el productor/la productora

profession la profesión

profit el beneficio

program el programa

prohibited prohibido/a

projector el proyector

promise la promesa

proposal la propuesta

prosper prosperar

protect proteger

protest (n.) la protesta

Protestant el/la protestante

proud orgulloso/a

public público/a

public bathroom los servicios, los aseos

pudding el budín, el pudín

pull tirar

pulpit el púlpito

pulse el pulso

pump la bomba

pumpkin la calabza

puncture el pinchazo

punish castigar

puppy el/la cachorro/a

pure puro/a

purple morado, violeta

push empujar

purse la bolsa

purser el sobrecargo, el contador

push empujar

put poner

put on ponerse

Q

qualifications la capacidad, el requisito

quality la calidad

quarrel la pelea, la riña

quarter cuarto

queen la reina

question (n.) la pregunta

question (v.) preguntar

quick rápido/a

quickly aprisa

quiet tranquilo/a

quinine la quinina

quit dejar

R

rabbit el conejo

race (breed) la raza

race (run) la carrera

racism el racismo

rack la red

racquet la raqueta

radiator el radiador

radio el radio

radishes los rábanos

raft la balsa

railroad el ferrocarril

railroad station la estación de tren

rain la lluvia

rainbow el arco iris

raincoat el impermeable

raining lloviendo

raisins las pasas

rare (meat) bien cruda

rare raro/a

rash la erupción

rash, diaper el escozor del pañal

raspberry la frambuesa

rat la rata

rate of pay el salario

rattle (for a baby) el sonajero

raw crudo/a

rayon el rayón

razor la navaja de afeitar

razor blade la hoja de afeitar

reach alcanzar

read leer

ready listo/a

realism el realismo

realize darse cuenta de

reason la razón, el motivo

receipt el recibo

receive recibir

recent reciente

recently recientemente

reception desk la recepción

receptionist el/la recepcionista

recipe la receta

recognize reconocer

recommend recomendar

recording la grabación

rectum el recto

recycling el reciclaje

red rojo/a

referee el árbitro

reference la referencia

refill el recambio

reflection el reflejo

refrigerator la nevera, el frigorífico, el refrigerador

refugee el/la refugiado/a

refund el reembolso

refuse negar

regards los recuerdos, los saludos

regional regional

registered certificado, registrado

regret lamentar

relationship la relación

relax relajar

relaxation la relajación

relic la reliquia

religion la religión

remember recordar

remote control el control remoto

Renaissance el Renacimiento

republic la república

rent alquilar

repair (n.) la reparación
repair (v.) arreglar, componer
repeat repetir
repellent el repelente
reservation la reserva
reserve reservar
respect (n.) el respeto
respect (v.) respetar
rest (relax) descanso
rest (remainder) el resto
rest (v.) descansar
restaurant el restaurante
resumé el currículum
retired jubilado/a
return volver
reverse reverso, dorso
rhythm el ritmo
rib la costilla
rich rico/a
ride montar
right (correct) correcto/a
right (direction) la derecha
right now ahora, en este momento
ring el anillo
ring (a telephone) sonar
ripe maduro/a
rip-off la estafa

risk el riesgo
river el río
road el camino, la carretera
roasted asado/a
rob robar
robe la bata
rock la roca
roll (n.) el bollo, el panecillo
roller coaster la montaña rusa
roller skates los patines
Romanesque románico
romance el amor
roof el techo
room la habitación, el cuarto
room service el servicio de habitaciones
rope la cuerda
rosemary el romero
rotten podrido/a
rouge el colorete
roundabout la glorieta
round trip ida y vuelta
rowboat el bote
ruby el rubí
rude descortés
rug la alfombra

223

ruins las ruinas
rules las reglas
run correr
Russia Rusia

S

sad triste
saddle el sillín
safe (adj.) seguro/a
safe (n.) la caja fuerte
safety pin el imperdible
sailboat el barco de vela
saint el/la santo/a
saint's day el día del santo
salad la ensalada
salami el salchichón
salary el salario
sale la venta
salesperson el vendedor, la vendedora
salmon el salmón
salt la sal
salt shaker el salero
same mismo/a
samples las muestras
sand la arena
sandals las sandalias
sandwich el sándwich, el bocadillo
sanitary napkins las toallas higiénicas, las compresas
Santa Claus Papá Noel
sardine la sardina
Saturday el sábado
sauce la salsa
sausage la salchicha, el chorizo
save (money) ahorrar
save (on computer) guardar, salvar
say decir
scandalous escandaloso/a
Scandinavia Escandinavia
scarf la bufanda
schedule el horario
school la escuela, el colegio
science la ciencia
scientist el/la científico/a
scissors las tijeras
score marcar
scotch tape la cinta adhesiva
Scotland Escocia
scrapbook el álbum de recortes
scratch (n.) el rasguño

screen (computer, etc.) la pantalla

screwdriver el destornillador

script el guión

sculpture la escultura

sea el mar

seafood los mariscos

search engine el navegador

seasick mareado/a

seaside la costa

seasons las estaciones

seat el asiento

seatbelt el cinturón de seguridad

second segundo/a

second-class la segunda clase

secret secreto

secretary el/la secretario/a

sedative el sedante

see ver

seem parecer

see you later hasta luego

see you tomorrow hasta mañana

selection (assortment) el surtido

selfish egoísta

self-service el auto-servico

sell vender

send enviar

seniors los ancianos

sensible juicioso/a

sentence la frase, la oración

September septiembre

series la serie

serious serio/a

seriously en serio, gravemente

serve servir

service el servicio

service charge pago de servicio

set fijar

several varios/as

sew coser

sex el sexo

sexy sexy

shade (not in the sun) la sombra

shade (tone) el tono

shadow la sombra

shady sombreado

shampoo el champú

shave afeitar

ENGLISH-SPANISH DICTIONARY

shaving cream la crema de afeitar

she ella

sheep la oveja

sheet la sábana

shell la concha

shelves las estanterías

sherbet el sorbete

sherry el jerez

shine (v.) brillar

ship (n.) el barco

ship (v.) enviar

shirt la camisa

shoe store la zapatería

shoelaces los cordones

shoes los zapatos

shoes, flats los bajos

shoes, high heels los tacones

shoes, tennis los tenis

shoot disparar

shop (n.) la tienda

shop, antique el anticuario

shop, barber la peluquería

shop, camera la tienda de fotos

shop, cell phone la tienda de teléfonos

shop, coffee la cafetería

shop, jewelry la joyería

shop, pastry la pastelería

shop, photocopy la tienda de fotocopias

shop, souvenir la tienda de recuerdos

shop, sweets la dulcería

shop, wine la tienda de vinos

shopping las compras

shopping mall el centro comercial

short bajo/a

shorts los shorts, los pantalones cortos

shorts (men's underwear) los calzoncillos

shortage la escasez

shoulder el hombro

shout gritar

show (n.) el espectáculo

show (v.) mostrar

shower (n.) la ducha

shower (v.) ducharse

shrimp los camarones, las gambas

shrine la capilla, el altar

shut cerrar

shy tímido/a

sick enfermo/a
side el lado
sidewalk la acera
sign la señal
sightseeing las visitas a puntos de interés
signature la firma
silence el silencio
silk la seda
silver la plata
similar similar, semejante
simple sencillo/a, simple
sin el pecado
since desde que
sing cantar
singer el/la cantante
single único, solo
single (room) sencillo/a
single person el soltero, la soltera
sink el lavabo
sink stopper el tapón
sinus problems la sinusitis
sir señor
sister la hermana
sit sentarse
size el tamaño
size of clothes la talla
size of shoes el número

skating el patinaje
ski esquiar
ski lift el telesquí
skillful hábil
skin la piel
skirt la falda
ski slope la pista
skull el cráneo
sky el cielo
sleep dormir
sleeper (train) el coche cama
sleeping bag el saco de dormir
sleeping pill la pastilla para dormir
sleepy tener sueño, soñoliento/a
sleeves las mangas
slice la rebanada
slip la combinación
slippers las zapatillas
slippery resbaladizo/a
slow lento/a, despacio/a
slower más lento, más despacio
slowly lentamente, poco a poco
sly astuto/a
small pequeño/a

ENGLISH-SPANISH DICTIONARY

smaller más pequeño/a
smell (n.) el olor
smell (v.) oler
smile (n.) la sonrisa
smile (v.) sonreír
smoke (n.) el humo
smoke (v.) fumar
smoker el fumador, la fumadora
snack el pincho, el refrigerio
snake la serpiente
sneeze (n.) el estornudo
sneeze (v.) estornudar
snore roncar
snorkel el tubo de buceo, el esnórkel
snow la nieve
soap el jabón
soap (for laundry) el detergente
soap opera la telenovela, el culebrón
soccer el fútbol
socks los calcetines
solid sólido/a
some algo/a
somebody alguien
sometimes de vez en cuando

something algo/a
son el hijo
song la canción
soon pronto
sore throat la inflamación de garganta
(I'm) sorry lo siento
sound el sonido
soup la sopa
sour amargo/a
south el sur
South America Sudamérica
souvenirs los recuerdos
space el espacio
Spain España
Spanish el español
spare de repuesta
sparkplugs las bujías
speak hablar
special especial
special delivery entrega inmediata
specialist el/la especialista
specialty la especialidad
speed la velocidad
speed limit el límite de velocidad
spell deletrear

spend gastar

spicy picante

spider la araña

spinach la espinaca

spine la espina

splint la tablilla

spoon la cuchara

sport el deporte

sprain la torcedura

spring (v.) brotar

spring season la primavera

square (place) la plaza

squash la calabaza

stable la cuadra, el establo

stadium el estadio

stage el escenario

stainless steel el acero inoxidable

stain remover el quitamanchas

stairs las escaleras

stall el puesto

stallion el semental

stamps la estampilla, el timbre, el sello

standard normal

standard of living el nivel de vida

stand someone up dejar plantado/a alguien

stapler la grapadora

star la estrella

start empezar, comenzar

state el estado

stateroom el camarote

station la estación

statue la estatua

stay (remain) quedarse

stay (somewhere) alojarse, hospedarse

steal robar

steam el vapor

steering wheel el volante

steep escarpado/a

step el paso

stepbrother el hermanastro

stepfather el padrastro

stepmother la madrastra

stepsister la hermanastra

stew el guiso, el guisado, el estofado, el cocido

steward el mayordomo

sting la picadura

stockings las medias

stomach el estómago

stone (precious) la piedra (preciosa)

stop (n.) la parada

ENGLISH-SPANISH DICTIONARY

stop (v.) parar
stoplight el semáforo
stopper el tapón
store la tienda
store, department el almacén
store, hardware la ferretería
store, toy la juguetería
stork la cigüeña
storm la tormenta
story (building) la planta
story (tale) el cuento
stove la estufa
straight derecho
straight ahead todo derecho, directo
strange extraño/a
stranger el/la extranjero/a
strap la correa
straw la paja
strawberry la fresa
stream el arroyo
street la calle
streetcar el tranvía
strength la fuerza
stretch estirarse
stretcher la camilla
strict estricto/a

strike la huelga
string la cuerda
striped a rayas
stroll (n.) el paseo
stroller el carrecoche, el cochecito
strong fuerte
stubborn testarudo/a, terso/a
stuck atascado/a
student el/la estudiante
studio el estudio
studious estudioso/a
study estudiar
suburb el barrio
suburbs of las afueras de
subtitle el subtítulo
subway el metro
subway entrance la entrada al metro
subway exit la salida del metro
subway map el mapa del metro
subway station la estación de metro
subway stop la parada del metro
success el éxito
suddenly de repente

suffer sufrir

sugar el azúcar

sugar bowl la azucarera

suit el traje

suitcase la maleta

suite la suite

summer el verano

sun el sol

sunbathe tomar el sol

sunblock el filtro solar, el bloqueador solar

Sunday el domingo

sunburn la quemadura de sol

sunburn ointment ungüento para quemadura de sol

sunflower oil el aceite de girasol

sunglasses las gafas de sol

sunny soleado/a

sunrise amancer

sunscreen el bronceador con filtro solar

sunset la puesta del sol

sunstroke la insolación

suntan el bronceado

suntan lotion el protector solar

supermarket el supermercado

supplement el suplemento

supporter los/las hinchas

sure (agreement) claro

surfboard la tabla de surf

surfer el/la surfista

surface la superficie

surname el apellido

surprise la sorpresa

survive sobrevivir

suspenders los tirantes

swallow (v.) tragar

sweat (v.) sudar

sweater el suéter, el jersey

sweet dulce

sweet shop la dulcería

swollen hinchado/a

swim nadar

swim trunks el bañador

swimsuit el traje de baño

swimming pool la piscina

Switzerland Suiza

sword la espada

sympathetic comprensivo/a

ENGLISH-SPANISH DICTIONARY

synagogue   la sinagoga
synthetic   el sintético
syrup (medicine)   el
  jarabe
syrup (sugary)   el
  almíbar
syringe   la jeringa

T

table   la mesa
tablespoonful   la cuchara
table tennis   el ping pong
tail   el rabo
taillights   la luz de frenoado
tailor (n.)   el sastre
take   tomar, llevar, coger
take away   llevar
take back   recuperar
take charge   encargar
take off (plane)
  despegar
taken   reservado
take-out (food)   la comida
  para llevar
talcum powder   los polvos
  de talco
talented   talentoso/a
talk   hablar
tall   alto/a
tampons   los tampones

tanning lotion   el
  bronceador
tap water   el agua del
  grifo
tape (adhesive)   la cinta
  adhesiva
tape (cassette)   el casete
tart   la tarta
tart (flavor)   agrio/a
taste (n.)   sabor
taste (v.)   probar
tasty   sabroso/a, rico/a
tax   el impuesto
taxi   el taxi
tea   el té
teacher   el profesor, la
  profesora
teaching   la enseñanza
team   el equipo
tears   las lágrimas
teaspoon   la cucharita
teaspoonful   la
  cucharadita
technique   la técnica
teddy bear   el osito de
  peluche
teenager   el/la joven
teeth   los dientes
teething   la dentición
telegram   el telegrama

telephone (n.) el teléfono

telephone (v.) llamar por teléfono

telephone card la tarjeta telefónica

telescope el telescopio

television la televisión

tell decir

temperature (fever) la fiebre

temperature (weather) la temperatura

temple el templo

temporarily por ahora

temporary temporal

tender tierno/a

tenderloin el filete

tendon el tendón

tennis el tenis

tennis shoes los zapatillos de tenis

tent la tienda de campaña

tent pegs las estacas de tienda

term of office el mandato

terrible terrible

test la prueba, el exámen

thanks gracias

theater el teatro

theme park el parque de atracciones

thermometer el termómetro

they ellos

there allí, acá

there is, there are hay

there was, there were hubo, había

thermometer el termómetro

thick grueso/a

thief el ladrón

thigh el muslo

thimble el dedal

thin flaco/a, delgado/a

thing la cosa

think pensar

third-class la tercera clase

thirsty sediento/a, tener sed

thoroughfare la vía pública

thought el pensamiento

thoughtful considerado/a

thread el hilo

thriller (movie) el cine de suspenso

throat la garganta

through a través

throw tirar
throw out echar
thumb el pulgar
Thursday el jueves
thyme el tomillo
ticket el billete, el pasaje, la entrada
tight ajustado/a, estrecho/a
tile, blue el azulejo
time el tiempo, la vez
time (on the clock) la hora
time, on puntual
timetable el horario
tin la lata
tip (for service) la propina
tire la llanta
tire (auto) el neumático
tired cansado/a
tired of harto/a
tissue el pañuelo de papel
to a
toad el sapo
toast la tostada
tobacco el tabaco
today hoy
toe el dedo del pie

together juntos/as
toilet el inodoro
toilet paper el papel higiénico
toilets (restrooms) los servicios
token la ficha
tolerant tolerante
toll el peaje
toll-free la llamada gratuita
tomato el tomate
tomorrow mañana
tomorrow afternoon mañana por la tarde
tomorrow morning mañana por la mañana
tomorrow, day after pasado mañana
tongue la lengua
tonight esta noche
tonsils las amígdalas
too también, demasiado
too much, too many demasiado/a
tools las herramientas
tooth el diente
tooth (molar) la muela
toothache el dolor de muelas

toothbrush el cepillo de dientes

toothpaste la pasta de dientes

toothpick el palillo

touch tocar

tour el viaje

tour, with guide una visita con guía

tourist el/la tourista

tough duro/a

tournament el torneo

tourniquet el torniquete

tow remolcar

tow truck el carro de remolque

towards hacia

towel la toalla

tower la torre

town el pueblo

toxic waste los residuos tóxicos

toy el juguete

toy store la juguetería

track (footprints) el rastro

track (path) el sendero

track (sports) la pista

traditional tradicional

traffic el tráfico

traffic light el semáforo

trail el sendero

train el tren

train car el vagón, el coche

tram el tranvía

transfer (n.) el transbordo

transfer (v.) cambiar

translate traducir

transmission fluid el líquido de transmisión

travel viajar

travel agency la agencia de viajes

traveler el/la viajero/a

traveler's checks los cheques de viajero

treasury el tesoro

tree el árbol

tremor el temblor

trendy moderno/a

trigonometry la trigonometría

trip (n.) el viaje

trip (v.) tropezar con

tripod el trípode

trouble la dificultad

trousers los pantalones

trout la trucha

truck   el camión

true   verdad

trunk   el baúl

trust (v.)   confiar

trust   la confianza

try   tratar

try on   probarse

T-shirt   la camiseta

Tuesday   el martes

tuna   el atún

tune   la melodía

tunnel   el túnel

Turkey   Turquía

turkey   el pavo, el guajolote

turn   doblar, dar una vuelta

turn signal   el intermitente

turnip   el nabo

TV   la tele

TV set   el televisor

tweezers   las pinzas

twice   dos veces

twin   el/la gemelo/a

twin bed   la cama gemela

type   escribir a máquina

typewriter   la máquina de escribir

typhoid   la fiebre tifoidea

typical   típico/a

U

ugly   feo/a

ultrasound   el ultrasonido

umbrella   el paraguas

unbearable   insoportable

uncle   el tío

unconscious   inconsciente

under   debajo

underpants (men)   los calzoncillos

underpants (women)   las bragas

underscore (_____)   el subrayado

undershirt   la camiseta

understand   comprender

underwear   la ropa interior

unemployed   sin empleo

unfortunate   desafortunado

United States   Estados Unidos

universe   el universo

university   la universidad

unleaded   sin plomo

unsafe   inseguro/a

until hasta
unusual extraño/a
up arriba
uphill cuesta arriba
upstairs de arriba
urgent urgente
urinary infection infección urinaria
us nosotros/as
U.S.A. Estados Unidos
USB port el puerto USB
use usar
useful útil
usher el acomodador

V

vacancy, no completo
vacancy sign habitaciones
vacant libre
vacation la vacación
vaccination la vacuna
valid válido/a
validate validar
valley el valle
valuable precioso/a
value el precio
van la caravana, la furgoneta
vase el florero

Vaseline la vaselina
veal la ternera
vegetable garden la huerta
vegetables los vegetales, las legumbres, las verduras
vegetarian vegetariano/a
vein la vena
velvet el terciopelo
venison el venado
venue el local
very muy
vest el chaleco
video el video
video camera la cámara de video
view la vista
village la aldea
vine la vid
vinegar el vinagre
vineyard el viñedo
violence la violencia
virus el virus
visa el visado
visit (n.) la visita
visit (v.) visitar
vitamins las vitaminas
voice la voz

volume el volumen
vomiting los vómitos
vote votar
vulture el buitre

W

waist la cintura
wait esperar
waiter el mesero, el camarero, el mozo
waiting room la sala de espera
waitress la mesera, la camarera, la moza
wake up despertarse
Wales País de Gales
walk (v.) andar, caminar
wall, fortified la pared fortificada
wall (inside) la pared
wall (outside) el mural
wall-to-wall carpeting la alfombra moqueta
wallet la billetera, la cartera
want querer
war la guerra
wardrobe el vestuario
warm caliente
warn advertir

wash lavar
washcloth la toallita
washer la lavadora
watch (n.) el reloj
watch (v.) mirar
water el agua
water bottle la cantimplora
water skiing el esquí acuático
water, potable el agua potable
water, tap el agua del grifo
waterfall la cascada
watermelon la sandía
wave la olla
wax la cera
way el camino
we nosotros/as
weak débil
wealthy rico/a
wear llevar
weather el tiempo
website la página de la red, el sitio web
wedding la boda
wedding anniversary el aniversario de bodas

wedding cake el pastel nupcial

wedding present el regalo de bodas

Wednesday el miércoles

week la semana

week, last la semana pasada

week, this esta semana

weekend el fin de semana

weigh pesar

weight el peso

welcome bienvenido

welfare el bienestar

well bien

well done bien hecho

west el oeste

wet mojado/a

what qué (question), que

wheel la rueda

wheelchair la silla de ruedas

wheelchair-accessible el acceso de silla de ruedas

when cuándo (question), cuando

where dónde (question), donde

while mientras

white blanco/a

who quién (question), quien

whole todo

why por qué (question)

wide ancho/a

widow la viuda

widower el viudo

width ancho

wife la esposa, la mujer

wild salvaje

wild animal el animal salvaje

win ganar

wind (breeze) el viento

windsurfing el windsurf

window la ventana

window (on plane or train) la ventanilla

window in a shop la vitrina

window shop mirar los escaparates

windshield el parabrisas

windshield washer el limpiaparabrisas

windy ventoso/a

wine el vino

wine shop la tienda de vinos

ENGLISH-SPANISH DICTIONARY

winery la bodega
wing el ala
winner el ganador, la ganadora
winter el invierno
wire el alambre
wise sabio/a
wish (v.) desear, querer
with con
within dentro de
without sin
wolf el lobo
woman la mujer
women las mujeres
wonderful estupendo/a, maravilloso/a
wood la madera
woodpecker el pájaro carpintero
wool la lana
word la palabra
word search la buscapalabras
work (n.) el trabajo
work (v.) trabajar
work permit el permiso de trabajo
workout el entrenamiento
workshop el taller
world el mundo

worm el gusano, la lombriz
worried peocupado/a
worse peor
worship la adoración
worth el valor
wound (injury) la herida
wrap envolver
wrench la llave inglesa
wrist la muñeca
wristwatch reloj de pulsera
write escribir
writer el escritor/la escritora
wrong equivocado/a
wrought iron window la reja

X

X-ray la radiografía

Y

yam el ñame
yawn el bostezo
year el año
year, last el año pasado
year, this este año
yellow amarillo/a
yes sí

yesterday   ayer
yesterday, day before
   anteayer
yet   todavía
yogurt   el yogur
you (formal)   usted
you (informal)   tú
you (plural)   ustedes
you (plural, informal in Spain)   vosotros/as
young   joven
youth   juventud

youth hostel   el albergue
   de juventud

Z

zebra   la cebra
zero   cero
zip code   el código postal
ziplock bag   la bolsa de
   cremallera
zipper   la cremallera
zoo   el zoo

INDEX

The words in capitals refer to sections, and the first number that follows (example: p. 81) refers to the page. Otherwise, ALL ENTRIES ARE INDEXED BY ITEM NUMBER.

INDEX